From Sandlots to League President

THE STORY OF JOE CRONIN

When Joe Cronin became President of the American League in 1960, he reached almost the top rung in a baseball career that covered thirty-five years. There was nothing in baseball, short of Commissioner, that he hadn't been—star shortstop, player-manager, field manager, general manager. And on the way up he won many honors, including the Most Valuable Player award and membership in baseball's Hall of Fame.

Books by Al Hirshberg

THE JACKIE JENSEN STORY

THE EDDIE MATHEWS STORY

THE MAN WHO FOUGHT BACK
Red Schoendienst

FROM SANDLOTS TO LEAGUE PRESIDENT
The Story of Joe Cronin

Owner Clark Griffith and Manager Joe Cronin of the Washington Senators (1933)

The versatile player-manager of the Boston Red Sox covering second base during spring training in Sarasota (1937)

Cronin helps his All-Stars win an exhibition game by hitting a home run (1935)

Managers Casey Stengel of the Boston Bees and Joe Cronin of the Boston Red Sox (1938)

Left to right: Bobby Doerr, Johnny Pesky, Cecil Hughson, Dave Ferris and Joe Cronin

Ted Williams and Joe Cronin (1941)

Cronin is being greeted by teammate Skeeter Newsome after pinch-hit homer (1943)

General Manager Joe Cronin surrounded by his family. Left to right, rear: Corky, 14 and Tom, 17; front: Joe Cronin, Kevin, 5, Mrs. Cronin, and daughter Maureen, 11 (1956)

Joe Cronin and Hank Greenberg with their Hall of Fame plaques (1956)

Ford Frick, baseball commissioner, Joe Cronin, new American League president and Will Harridge, retiring American League president (1959)

From Sandlots to League President

THE STORY OF JOE CRONIN

by

Al Hirshberg

 Julian Messner, Inc.

New York

Published by Julian Messner, Inc.
8 West 40 Street, New York 18

Published simultaneously in Canada
by The Copp Clark Publishing Co. Limited

Second Printing, 1962

Printed in the United States of America
Library of Congress Catalog Card No. 62-10197

To my secretary,
who doubles as my wife

From
Sandlots
to
League President

THE STORY OF JOE CRONIN

1.

It was a warm Indian summer afternoon in 1934, and Washington, D.C., a lovely city under any conditions, was at its brilliant best. Nevertheless, all the beauty of the nation's capital was lost on Clark Griffith, the blue-eyed, beetle-browed, grizzled owner of the Washington Senators. Oblivious to his surroundings, he sat in his office at the ball park, staring into space as he wrestled with the toughest problem of his forty years in baseball.

What should he do about Joe Cronin?

Here was one of the finest young men he had ever known, a great ballplayer, a pennant-winning big league manager at twenty-six, a clean-living, clear-thinking credit to the game who now, to Griffith's delight, had come into the family only a few weeks before. On September 27, Joe had married Mildred Robertson, Griffith's niece, and the old man himself had given her away, for she had grown up in his home and was like a daughter to him.

Griffith had great plans for Joe. He had wanted the man whom he now considered his son-in-law to take over this

9

ball club someday. He knew Cronin was capable of handling the job. Hadn't the youth brought the Senators a pennant the very first year he became their manager? Wasn't he the finest shortstop in baseball, a self-made hitter, a keen handler of men, a manager who had already fulfilled his potential? And now that he was a member of the Griffith family, wouldn't he make a fine president for this ball club when the time came?

This last thought had been going through Griffith's mind almost since the first year Cronin had played ball for him. It began to crystallize when the old man watched the romance develop between Joe and Mildred right in this very office. Mildred was Griffith's secretary, and Cronin had found dozens of excuses for dropping by, even before he became manager. As head man, Joe didn't need any excuses; his own office was right next to Griffith's.

Originally, Mildred and Joe had intended to wait until the end of the baseball season before getting married, but on Labor Day Joe had broken his wrist in a game against the Boston Red Sox, and that finished him for the year as a player. Of course, he planned to stay with the ball club as the manager until the season was over.

The Senators, however, plagued by injuries, had sunk to seventh place, and showed no signs of climbing out. Knowing how eager Mildred and Joe were to get married, Griffith himself had suggested the earlier date, pointing out that one of the coaches could manage the ball club in the meaningless final week of the season. The young couple had jumped at the chance to be married sooner than they expected. After the ceremony, they immediately left for a leisurely honeymoon to San Francisco, Joe's home town, where they intended to live permanently.

When it was all over, Griffith had been at peace with the world. He rejoiced in his foster daughter's happiness and was

10

already thinking of plans for the 1935 baseball season. He planned to build a new club around Joe Cronin, and start the Senators back on the road toward the pennant they had won in 1933. He and Joe would be in touch with each other by telephone, and perhaps they could make some deals in December during the winter baseball meetings.

Then suddenly the bombshell struck—a bombshell which Griffith knew might well be a blessing in disguise. As he thought things over in his ball park office that October afternoon, he realized he should have been prepared for it. On the day Joe Cronin broke his wrist, Griffith had been given a broad hint of what was to come, but he passed it off as nothing more than a vague possibility.

The Red Sox were in town for a Labor Day weekend series, and, as often happened in those days, Tom Yawkey, the wealthy young Boston owner, was traveling with his ball club. So was Eddie Collins, the Red Sox vice-president and general manager. In the two years since he acquired the ball club, Yawkey had already electrified the baseball world with his openhanded purchases. Although the country was in the depths of the great depression, Yawkey had spent half a million dollars on ballplayers and was ready to spend more in his quest for a pennant.

Sitting in his office, Griffith recalled with distaste a story which had appeared in one of the Washington newspapers on Labor Day. It had read, in effect: "In spite of the fact that Joe Cronin may soon marry into the Griffith family, the old man is reported to be ready to sell him to the highest bidder and bring in a more mature manager. The same team that won the 1933 pennant will be seventh in 1934, and who but the manager can be blamed for it?"

The item had upset Griffith because it came right out of a reporter's head. Griffith had neither the desire nor the intention of selling Cronin, and he wasted no time saying so.

11

But his denial wouldn't get into print until after the holiday doubleheader. In the meantime, the original story would go out on the wires, and the whole baseball world would think he wanted to sell the man who would soon become his own son-in-law.

That very afternoon Yawkey and Collins had approached him at the ball park. As they sat in Griffith's box, Yawkey remarked, "Griff, I see by the papers that you're ready to sell Joe Cronin. We'd like to buy him."

"The papers were wrong," Griffith retorted gruffly. "Joe Cronin isn't for sale."

"Not even if the price is right?" asked the young Boston magnate.

"Cronin's not for sale," the old man repeated. "That's final."

And that, as far as Griffith knew, was the end of it. He and Yawkey and Collins sat through the two games, passing the time of day. Neither the Red Sox executives nor the Washington owner again mentioned Joe Cronin's name that afternoon.

But what Griffith didn't know was that Yawkey had no intention of dropping the subject. On the contrary, the more he thought about it, the better he liked the idea of bringing Joe Cronin to Boston. Cronin was Yawkey's kind of ballplayer—young, smart and aggressive. Perhaps beyond everything else, from Yawkey's point of view, Cronin was a baseball star, and Yawkey had been a hero-worshiper of baseball stars for as long as he could remember.

His ambition was to surround himself with them. He already had a few stars on the Red Sox, and he expected to get more in his quest for an American League pennant. Money was no object. He was ready to go high for Joe Cronin. Furthermore, he wanted the young shortstop to manage the Boston club.

Actually, the Red Sox already had a manager—Bucky Harris, one of the best, but Yawkey felt that young Cronin as player-manager would better fit into his plans for building up the club.

"Bucky won't have any trouble getting another job," Yawkey commented to Collins. "The big problem is how to get Cronin away from the Senators. I suppose I can't really blame Griff for not wanting to let him go. He's a great ballplayer and a great manager."

"He'd be the perfect manager for the Red Sox," Collins agreed. "He's a fighting Irishman, and Boston's the biggest Irish town in America. The fans here would fall in love with him."

"I know," Yawkey nodded. "Tell you what, Eddie. When we get to the World Series, let's offer Griffith so much money for Cronin that he *can't* refuse."

The 1934 World Series between the St. Louis Cardinals and the Detroit Tigers opened in Detroit. On the night before the first game, Griffith's phone rang at his Book-Cadillac Hotel suite.

"This is Tom Yawkey," the caller said. "Can you come up here?"

When Griffith arrived, Yawkey and Collins were waiting for him. Without a preliminary word, Yawkey said, "Griff, I'll give you a quarter of a million dollars for Joe Cronin."

Griffith, overwhelmed and stunned, stared at the young Red Sox owner. A quarter of a million dollars! Never in baseball history had such an offer been made for a single ballplayer. Only a handful had attracted as much as a hundred thousand.

As Griffith, unbelieving, looked at the smiling Yawkey, the thought of what a quarter of a million dollars could buy for his ball club flashed through his mind. The 1934 season had been disastrous for the Senators. They had lost all they

13

had won in the previous season—and then some. One of Griffith's problems in his plans for rebuilding had been basic and fundamental—where would he get the money to do the rebuilding?

In a weak voice he protested, "You can't be serious, Tom!"

"But I *am* serious," was the reply. "If I weren't, I wouldn't make the offer."

"I can't let you have Cronin," Griffith said slowly. "He's my son-in-law. I have big plans for him."

"We've got bigger ones," Yawkey told him in a quietly persuasive voice. "We'll give him a ten-thousand-dollar raise and a long-term contract."

"I've got to think it over. Give me some time."

"Take all the time you need, Griff," Yawkey said.

Now, with the World Series over, Griffith was still thinking it over, and he still could not definitely make up his mind. Since the Cronins were traveling, he hadn't been able to reach Joe. Under any circumstances, Griffith had no intention of making the deal without telling Cronin first. He didn't want the young man to find out about it in the newspapers.

All during the long Indian summer day, Griffith tried to find an answer to the problem. It wasn't the sort of thing he could talk over with anyone else. This was something he had to work out for himself.

Late that afternoon Eddie Collins called him from Boston.

"We're not trying to rush you, Griff," Collins said, "but we've got to know pretty soon what you've decided. We don't want to go to the winter meetings without knowing who our manager will be."

"Neither do I," Griffith replied. Then he said, "Y'know, if I let Joe go, I've got to find a new shortstop as well as a manager."

"You'll have a quarter of a million dollars to play with," Collins pointed out.

"A big league shortstop would come high," Griffith said. "How about throwing in Lary?"

"Lary's not just a big league shortstop," Collins objected. "He's one of the best in the business."

"And what'll you use him for if you have Cronin?" In spite of himself, Griffith was now bargaining, and there was nothing the Washington owner enjoyed more. He hadn't won the sobriquet, "the Old Fox," for nothing. Collins was quite right about Lyn Lary; the boy couldn't hit as well as Cronin, but he was nearly as slick a fielder.

"We can get some pretty good ballplayers for him," Collins retorted. Then, after a pause, the Red Sox executive cautiously asked, "Griff, if we throw in Lary, will you close the deal?"

"I'll let you know," Griffith answered. "I want to talk to Joe first."

After he hung up, the old man felt better. Much as he wanted to keep Cronin, it was time to think in practical terms. There were so many more arguments in favor of the deal than there were against it that he knew now he would have to agree to it. A quarter of a million dollars was an awful lot of money and Lyn Lary was an awful lot of shortstop. And there was no doubt about Yawkey's ability to do more for Joe Cronin than Griffith could himself.

Three days later, Griffith finally got hold of his new son-in-law and told him the whole story. When he finished, he said, "Joe, I'm going ahead with it. I think it's to the best interests of us all."

"Whatever you want to do is all right with me, Griff," the younger man said.

The next morning, Clark Griffith phoned Tom Yawkey and

15

the deal was made. It was confirmed a few days after that by the following letter, dated October 25, 1934:

Clark Griffith
Washington Baseball Club
Washington, D.C.
Dear Mr. Griffith:

The Boston American League Baseball Club agrees to give $250,000 and the contract of Lyn Lary for the contract of player-manager Joe Cronin, provided Cronin is satisfied by the terms submitted by Boston. Contract to be closed at convenience of parties after November 30, 1934, by execution of formal contract and the payment of $100,000 in cash, remainder of cash consideration at convenience of Boston club, prior to March 1, 1935 but after January 1, 1935.

Boston American League BB Club
Thomas A. Yawkey, Pres.

Joe Cronin, the son of a San Francisco truck driver, thus became the most expensive ballplayer of all time. He had come a long way since the days he was growing up on the streets and playgrounds of the city of his birth.

2.

The tiny house on Twenty-ninth Street, in the far Mission district of San Francisco, was so crowded that everyone was constantly getting into everyone else's way. Built many years before for one small family, it was now temporarily housing two—and the second family, while not large, was hardly small either. Jeremiah Cronin had moved in on his oldest sister Hannah Coughlan just a few months before, bringing with him his wife Mary, who was expecting a new baby, and his two sons. As soon as he could raise a little money, Jerry would have a place of his own again.

His sister didn't mind the inconvenience. It had been her idea that Jerry and his family share her home until he could get back on his feet. It was 1906, and the Cronins had lost their house and practically everything in it in the great earthquake of the previous April. The only thing they had saved was a rocking chair, but they considered themselves lucky. Nearly five hundred people had died in the disaster.

The baby arrived on October 12. Husky and square-jawed like his father, blue-eyed like his mother, Joseph

Edward Cronin was pure Irish on both sides of his family. His father had been born in county Cork in Ireland. His mother, whose maiden name was Mary Carolin, was a San Franciscan by birth, but her mother had been a Kelly from county Athlone in the old country.

Jerry Cronin didn't make much money, but at least he had a steady job driving a team of horses, and his family never starved. Ray and Jim, his two older boys, helped as soon as they were big enough, finding ways of making a few pennies here and there—shining shoes, running errands, selling newspapers and doing any other odd jobs suitable for youngsters.

Soon after Joe was born, Mr. Cronin found the house he was looking for at 412 Persia Avenue, in the Excelsior district, which, while well within the city limits, was really out in the country. It was a neighborhood of truck farms and inexpensive little houses, occupied by working people, all in similar financial circumstances. Although there were no sewers or sidewalks and the streets were unpaved, in common with every other neighborhood in town the district had its own playground. The Excelsior playground was just half a block from where the Cronins lived.

Because of its extensive facilities for children of all ages, San Francisco was a wonderful place in which to grow up. There were playgrounds everywhere, and so many local rivalries that it was hard to keep up with them all. The day never went by that Joe didn't compete in some sport—not only in baseball, his favorite, but in soccer, basketball, tennis and foot racing.

No matter what the boys played, however, their favorite talking sport was always baseball. Their hero was a slugging outfielder for the Chicago White Sox named Ping Bodie, who later starred for the New York Yankees in the early days of Babe Ruth's reign as the home run king. Bodie was a local boy who had played for the San Francisco Seals, and the Seals meant more than any major league team to the kids of the Bay Area.

Joe and his pals weren't the only ones who had their baseball heroes. Before Joe was old enough to play on an organized team, his father told him about his own favorites. One was Clark Griffith. After the 1893 season was over, Mr. Cronin told the youngster, Griffith and two other big league ballplayers organized an all-star team from the East, and took it to San Francisco to play an all-star team from the West. They didn't make enough money to get home, so the team disbanded and everyone went on his own. Griffith and another player earned their train fare working as black-faced end men in a Barbary Coast minstrel show.

Joe never forgot that story. From then on, Clark Griffith was one of his own heroes, and the Washington Senators one of his favorite teams.

Joe's closest friend was Jake Ward, who lived next door. Like Joe, he was practically born with a baseball glove in his hand. The two boys did everything together right up to their high school days—and they never stopped dreaming about baseball.

"Someday," Joe never tired of repeating, "I'm going to be a professional ballplayer."

"And I'll be right with you," Jake always nodded. "We'll be the stars of the Seals, and every kid in San Francisco will wish he were us."

"The Seals—"

With shining eyes, Joe would look toward Twin Peaks and murmur, "Just imagine, Jake—you and me playing for the Seals!"

It was good to dream, but the stark realities of life brought their daily pressures, and Joe had to sacrifice dreaming for finding ways to earn money. He delivered newspapers, ran

19

errands and did odd jobs wherever he could find them. However, nothing pleased him more than to work for Miss Stella Harris, the director of the Excelsior playground.

One day, when he was about nine years old, he arrived at the playground a little ahead of the other kids, and found her rolling the baseball diamond. She noticed him watching her as he stood along the first base line, and when she reached him she said, "How would you like to help me, Joe?"

"What do you want me to do?" the boy asked.

"Well, you can push one side of the roller while I push the other," she suggested. "I can use a boy with good muscles. I'll give you two cents."

"Okay," Joe said.

So he walked solemnly beside her, his hands just about reaching the handle of the roller as they marched around the dusty infield. Actually, Joe did very little pushing himself. He was neither tall enough nor strong enough to be of any real help, but it made him feel important, and he was very happy to get the two pennies when the job was done.

Joe always arrived at the playground early after that, and Miss Harris, who liked the earnest youngster with the determined jaw, generally managed to find something for him to do. As he grew older, he became really useful to her, and she made him her regular assistant when he was thirteen. At that point, Joe participated in almost every sport, often playing baseball, soccer and tennis all on the same day. He was equally good at everything he tried.

In 1919 Joe won the playground tennis title and with it the right to represent Excelsior in the city-wide boys' championship matches. On the day he was to play his first match, Miss Harris gave him a new pair of sneakers.

"What are these for?" he asked.

"You can't wear your old sneakers for the tournament,"

20

she said. "You'll trip all over them. So I want you to wear these. Maybe they'll bring you good luck."

Donning his new sneakers with pride and gratitude, Joe won the city championship hands down.

But nothing could take the place of baseball in his heart. His ambition was to become a big league ballplayer in the summer and a playground director like Miss Harris in the winter. Even at thirteen, he knew he must watch the professional ballplayers in action if he were to learn the game properly.

Charlie Graham, the owner of the Seals, wanted to stimulate the youngsters' interest in his ball club, and so every Friday, he permitted two children from each of the San Francisco public schools to get into Seals' games free. At the Cleveland School, which Joe attended, the teacher set up a merit badge system for good behavior during the week. The winners got the free tickets.

Although Joe Cronin was ordinarily no more angelic than any normal youngster of eighth-grade age, when the new system went into effect he suddenly became a model pupil. Week after week, he won one of the tickets and rushed off to Seals Stadium with the other winner—it was usually a boy named Al Scully—to sit in the bleachers, munch peanuts and thrill to the baseball skills of their favorites.

Joe loved them all, but he spent most of his time watching the shortstops. He always played shortstop in the daily ball games at Excelsior, and anywhere else he could find a pickup game. He learned to scoop up hot grounders off infields pockmarked with holes and filled with pebbles. Almost any ball was sure to take a bad hop, and Joe learned to expect it. As a result, his reflexes became so sharp, he could shift his hands in a split second when the ball took a sudden bounce in a new direction.

After he graduated from the Cleveland School, Joe went

21

on to Mission High, where he made the baseball team in his freshman year. Elmer Harris, the coach, put him at short-stop with the comment, "Anyone who can grab ground balls the way you do belongs on my team, no matter how young he is." Among Joe's teammates at Mission were Wally Berger, a future National League home run king, Jack Shelly, a future United States congressman, and Benny Lom, a future Rose Bowl football star.

Near the end of Joe's sophomore year, he and his class-mates saw a small boy's dream come true—the school burned down. It was too late to make other arrangements for classes, so the kids got an early summer vacation. For Joe, this meant that much more time for baseball. Not only did he play for the Excelsior team and other sandlot clubs around the city, he also found time to hold down his playground job.

September and the reopening of school came all too quickly. The new Mission High building wasn't ready for occupancy and so classes were held in a nearby church. When Joe got home from school after his first day, his mother asked him where classes were held.

"In a church down the street from Mission," he told her.

"A church?" Mrs. Cronin asked suspiciously. "What kind of a church?"

"A Protestant church," Joe said.

His mother sniffed. "A *Protestant* church?" she repeated in an outraged voice. "What would Father Ryan say? Joseph, we'll have no more of this Protestant church business. To-morrow you'll start going to a good Catholic school."

The next day Joe entered the Christian Brothers School of the Sacred Heart, where he remained for his final two years of high school.

Among other things, the change meant a new ball club for Joe. He knew most of the kids at Sacred Heart, since many of them either lived in the same neighborhood as he did or were fellow parishioners at the Church of the Epiphany. The boys on the ball club were among his best friends, for he had played with or against every one of them on one team or another.

Joe also played basketball and soccer at Sacred Heart, starring in both sports. His basketball ability helped him to get work as a referee. During the winter there were dozens of school and club and industrial games going on, and officials were always in demand. Even before Joe got out of high school, he was earning an average of five dollars a game.

During the summer of 1923, between his junior and senior years in high school, Joe eagerly accepted an invitation to join the Columbia Park Boys Club, which had the best team in the San Francisco *Examiner's* sandlot baseball league. The club, run by an enterprising promoter and philanthropist named Major Sidney Piexotto, was not only a consistent winner, but its members had many other benefits not ordinarily available to sandlot ballplayers.

The Major sponsored a gym team and a sixty-five-piece band which he took on an annual summer trip down the Pacific coast as soon as the sandlot season was over. The ballplayers went along, meeting local semipro teams in exhibition games wherever the troupe went. Nobody got any money, but everyone had a free vacation. And because the team was so good, it was an excellent springboard into professional baseball, since big league scouts always kept an eye on it.

The *Examiner* gave a Bill Doak glove to every boy on the championship team. Doak was a big league pitcher who, because of this prize, was as famous in San Francisco as in St. Louis, where he played for the Cardinals. Joe had yearned for a Bill Doak glove for years. He finally got one as the Columbia Park Boys Club shortstop when it won the *Examiner* title as usual.

Joe really looked forward to the trip, for it was the first time in his life he ever left the San Francisco Bay Area. The group traveled in a truck, hitting the small towns between San Francisco and Los Angeles. Everyone took part in the club's parade and band concert, which ballyhooed the ball game and the show that followed. In common with most of his teammates, Joe couldn't play any musical instrument, but the boys were all given one to carry in the parade. Joe had a saxophone, which he held to his mouth, but he never blew a note.

When Joe said good-by to Major Piexotto after the club arrived home, the Major said, "Don't ever give up baseball, Joe. You're going to be a big league ballplayer before you know it."

"Do you really think so?" Joe asked.

"I *know* it!" the other exclaimed.

When Joe got into a streetcar to go home to Persia Avenue, he was grinning from ear to ear. All the way, he sat pounding his Bill Doak glove and daydreaming about the day he would use it in the big leagues.

3.

By the spring of Joe's senior year in high school, he ranked as one of the finest schoolboy athletes in the San Francisco Bay Area. At seventeen Joe was a tall, skinny kid who stood nearly six feet in height and weighed less than one hundred and forty pounds, but his appearance was deceiving. Despite his build, he was supple and strong, with sure hands, powerful wrists and a throwing arm like a whiplash. Graceful and fast on his feet, he helped his school win city titles in both baseball and basketball.

In April Slip Madigan, the athletic director and football coach at St. Mary's College in nearby Moraga, was in San Francisco to interview boys for sports scholarships. Sacred Heart was one of his first stops, and, at his request, Joe was called out of class to talk to him.

"How would you like to go to college?" Madigan asked.

"Gee, I don't know," Joe replied. "I never thought much about it."

"We'll give you a basketball and baseball scholarship if you'd like to come to St. Mary's," Madigan told him.

"Well, that's sure nice of you and I appreciate it," the boy said. "But I don't know what to tell you. The folks need every cent we can pick up and I wouldn't be able to make much at college."

"Talk it over with them," Madigan said, "and then let me know when you decide what to do."

After several family conferences, Joe's brother Ray said, "I think it would be a good thing for Joe to go, but maybe we ought to wait and see what comes up. After all, we don't have to do anything about it until the end of the summer."

Joe secretly breathed a sigh of relief, for he had no great desire to spend the next four years on a college campus. He might be in the big leagues by that time if he turned out to be as good as everyone seemed to think. He could prove it only by playing against professional ballplayers, not college boys, and he'd be able to send money home at the same time. He made up his mind not to go to St. Mary's unless the family insisted.

In the meantime, baseball took up most of his time. The high school team came first, but he also played for three or four different sandlot teams. Then, just before he was graduated, he got a chance to play for Napa, a club in the fastest semipro league around San Francisco. All the players were grown men, but Joe didn't worry about that. The only thing that concerned him was his amateur standing because he still had a few school games to play. He got around that by being Joe Cronin around San Francisco and using the name "Joe Smith" around Napa, where he collected seven-fifty a game. He knew he was doing the wrong thing; he worried about being found out, but he reasoned that the extra money was needed so badly at home that it outweighed any possible wrong.

On the day after he was graduated, Joe regained his real name and demanded a raise in pay. Despite the fact that he

26

was the youngest man on the team, he was already the Napa star. The coach, Tom Phelan, upped his fee to twelve-fifty a game. Between that and a new job in the playground system, Joe made a fairly good week's pay that summer.

The semipro season reached its climax in early August. By then, Napa and San Mateo were battling for the championship, and the Bay Area fans were all steamed up. As the leading batter in the league, Joe was a popular hero, but so was Bud DeMeyer, a boy his age who pitched for San Mateo. The rivalry between the two youngsters had captured the imagination of fans and players everywhere around San Francisco.

Napa and San Mateo were to meet in a twilight game on a Tuesday at San Mateo, which was a few miles down the peninsula from San Francisco—a twenty-five-cent streetcar ride from the Cronins' house. Since the game would decide the league championship, it created so much local excitement that Joe's parents, who had never seen him play, decided to go.

However, Joe sprained his ankle in a game at Napa on the previous Sunday and by the time he got off the boat after crossing the bay to San Francisco, he could hardly walk. Instead of going home, he went over to Tom Phelan's house, and the Napa coach spent half the night putting hot compresses on the bad ankle. Then Joe went home and continued treating it all day Monday, Monday night and all Tuesday morning. He not only got very little sleep, but the ankle showed only a slight improvement, and game time found him sitting unhappily on the bench.

The contest turned into a pitching duel, reading a scoreless tie by Napa's half of the ninth inning. Then, with two out, Napa got men on first and second base with the pitcher coming up. In common with many pitchers, he was a poor hitter and everybody knew it.

Tom Phelan looked over at Joe and asked, "Do you think you could go up there and swing a bat?"

"I'd sure like to try," Joe replied.

"Well, go ahead then," the coach said.

Joe hobbled to the plate, and stood facing his friend Bud DeMeyer on the San Mateo mound. Always a fidgety batter, Joe, among other things, had a habit of hitching up his pants between swings. While standing at the plate, he wiggled his bat, moved around the batter's box until the last minute, looking like a model for a perpetual motion machine.

The count went to three and two, then Bud threw a fast ball. Joe leaned heavily into it off his good foot and belted it on a line between the center and left fielders. The two had to chase it so far that, with two good legs, Joe could have gone all the way around the bases. However, in swinging at the pitch he had put pressure on his bad ankle, and while the men on base scampered home, Joe barely managed to hobble to first before the ball was relayed in from the outfield.

He was suffering intense pain but was very happy. His hit had won the title for Napa.

When he got home that night, his mother scolded him for not telling her about his ankle. Then without giving him an opportunity to explain, she said, "Here," and handed him a safety pin.

"What's that for?" he asked.

"To hold up your pants," she replied. "The way you kept pulling at them, I was afraid you were going to lose them in front of all those people."

The publicity on Joe's pinch hit was terrific. His name was in sports page headlines the next day, and one of the papers ran his picture. Before the day was over, Joe Devine, a scout from the Pittsburgh Pirates, made a date to see Joe with his family at home that night, and Charlie Graham called to talk to him about playing for the Seals.

When Mrs. Cronin heard that two different clubs were after him, she was amazed.

"Do you mean to tell me these people will really pay you for playing ball?" she demanded.

"They sure will, Mom," Joe said.

"How much?"

"I don't know, but we'll soon find out."

That night Devine came and sat around for a couple of hours talking about the Pittsburgh ball club. He made such a deep impression that none of the Cronins realized until after he left that he hadn't actually made an offer.

"I don't know what Mr. Graham might have to say," Ray commented, "but I think the best thing for you to do, Joe, is sit around and wait a little while. It's too late to do anything for this year anyhow. The season's practically over."

"I've always wanted to play for the Seals," Joe said.

"The Seals aren't the Pirates," his brother pointed out. "Even if they should offer more money, they're still the minor leagues."

As they talked, their mother looked in wonder from one to the other. "My goodness," she exclaimed, "this is the craziest thing I ever heard of. You boys are talking about baseball just as if it were a business."

"It *is* a business, Mom," said Joe.

"Well," Mrs. Cronin remarked, "it still seems like a game to me. And I'm not so sure I want you associating with sporting characters all your life. I think you ought to get a job just like everybody else."

She maintained this attitude all during the next month while Joe was trying to make up his mind whether to sign with the Seals or the Pirates. The whole family had agreed to rule out college, especially since it didn't mean enough to Joe to make the necessary sacrifices it would take for him to go there. He wrote to Madigan, thanking him but turning down the St. Mary's scholarship offer.

Finally Charlie Graham promised to pay Joe three hundred dollars a month to play for the Seals. Joe was just about ready to accept when Joe Devine phoned.

"Can you meet me at Klawan and McMullen's at two o'clock this afternoon?" the scout asked.

"I'll be there," Joe said.

Klawan and McMullen's, a sporting goods store at the corner of Mission and Fourth in downtown San Francisco, was a meeting place for everyone in town interested in sports. Records were kept, schedules were made—and news broke there. Joe always dropped in once or twice a week during the summer to see what was going on. Devine was waiting for him when he arrived that afternoon.

"The Pirates will give you two hundred dollars to sign now and four hundred a month, starting next season," Devine said bluntly.

Joe stared, his eyes shining and his heart beating fast. *The Pirates not only wanted him, but would pay more than the Seals!* Joe had to fight an impulse to shout *"Yes!"* He was sure his brother and his parents would want him to accept, but his native caution and family training made him hesitate. Instead of grabbing Devine's offer on the spot, Joe, trying to sound as casual as possible, asked, "Can I let you know tonight?"

"Sure," the scout said. "I'll call you around nine."

Joe walked out of the store, but the minute he was outside he started running for a streetcar. All the way home, his heart continued to pound, as he whispered over and over, "The Pirates . . . the . . . Pirates . . . the Pirates. . . ."

He burst into the little house on Persia Avenue, yelling, "Mom—I've great news! The Pirates offered me a contract!"

"You mean they really—?"

"They want to give me two hundred dollars now," he cried breathlessly, "and four hundred a month starting next spring."

"My heavens," she exclaimed, half to herself. "Who would have believed it?" Then she said, "That's a terrible lot of money, Joe. I'm not sure you should take it. What kind of people will you be meeting?"

"Well, Mom—"

"I'm going over to see Father Ryan," Mrs. Cronin interrupted. "I want to know what he thinks about this."

At the church rectory, she told the priest what had happened, then asked if Joe should accept the Pirates' offer.

"Mrs. Cronin," Father Ryan said gravely, "in all my life I have never heard happier news told in a sadder way. Why, this is the greatest thing that could happen, and I'm tickled to death for Joe. Don't you worry. He's going to be a fine ballplayer."

"Yes, but the men he'll be associated with—" she began.

The priest held up his hand. "The people he'll associate with will be boys just like himself," he said. "Is that bad?"

"No, Father, I guess it isn't," she admitted.

"Mrs. Cronin, you go on home and don't worry about a thing. This is a wonderful opportunity for Joe, and I'm sure he'll take advantage of it. And, believe me, it won't be long before you're the proudest mother in all San Francisco."

That night Joe agreed to sign with the Pirates. The kid from Persia Avenue was a full-fledged professional ballplayer, and he hadn't yet turned eighteen. Not only that, but he could contribute substantially to the family treasury. The two hundred dollars he received from the Pirates was immediately applied toward the mortgage on the Cronin house.

31

4.

THE SECOND TRIP JOE CRONIN EVER MADE AWAY FROM HOME
was to report to the Pirates at their spring training camp at
Paso Robles, California, in 1925. He had made the first
trip in a truck with the Columbia Park Boys Club. He took
this one in a train with a boy his own age named Eddie
Montague, who had also been signed to a Pittsburgh contract by Joe Devine. The two had played against each other
often, both in high school and on the sandlots. Eddie had
gone to Polytechnical High, and also played for the Sunset
Federals in the *Examiner* League.

"I wonder where they'll send us," Joe said as the train
pulled away from the Sante Fe railroad station in San
Francisco.

"A million to one we won't see Pittsburgh this year," Eddie commented.

Joe sighed. "I suppose not, but I sure hope to see Pittsburgh soon."

Pittsburgh turned out to be a long way from Paso Robles
in more ways than one. The Pirates, who had finished third

in the 1924 pennant race, were a powerful team, managed by Bill McKechnie, one of the shrewdest field bosses in baseball at the time. Joe had little hope of sticking with the ball club, but he had reserved the right to dream. All winter long he had imagined himself looking so good that McKechnie would say, "Son, you're my shortstop because you're better even than Glenn Wright." The Pirates would trade Wright, and the job would be Joe's.

But it didn't work out quite that way. Neither McKechnie nor anyone else paid much attention to Joe at Paso Robles. Wright, a smooth, graceful infielder and a fine hitter, was one of the best shortstops in the game, and an eighteen-year-old without a day of organized baseball experience behind him didn't have a chance.

"If they'd only look at me," Joe said to Eddie Montague, who roomed with him, "maybe I could prove something."

"They won't look at me either," the other remarked. "I guess they're just not interested in kids like us."

A few days later, during batting practice, Joe moved over to take a ground ball but it hopped off his glove and bounded into the outfield.

"Try it this way, kid," someone said.

Joe turned—and there was Glenn Wright, bending down with his arms extended, showing him how to make the play. Joe, mumbling his thanks, tried to copy the shortstop. Wright grinned. "That's the stuff," the veteran said. "You'll get it."

Not long after that, an elderly man with clear blue eyes and a weather-beaten face, whom Joe had admired from a distance, called him aside and remarked, "I like your attitude, kid. You've got a long way to go, but if you really work at it you might be a first-class hitter someday."

"Gee, thanks, Mr. Clarke," Joe said. "I sure appreciate that." Then, with a big grin on his face, he watched Fred Clarke, one of the great ballplayers at the turn of the century, walk away. Clarke, who had managed four Pirate teams to pennants in the years between 1901 and 1909, was a club executive now, but Joe thought of him only as a ballplayer and manager.

Back in the room that night, Joe said, "Eddie—Fred Clarke spoke to me today. Imagine him having time for a kid like me!"

By this time both boys were reconciled to the prospect of being farmed out. Montague, a third baseman, had no more chance to make the team than Joe, for the Pirates had the greatest hot corner guardian in the business in Pie Traynor. It was just a question of time when the kids from San Francisco would be sent elsewhere.

They were still with the Pirates, however, when the club broke camp to go east. Neither got into any exhibition games for more than an inning or two, but, contrary to their expectations, they actually did see Pittsburgh. They found a room near Forbes Field and wondered how much longer they would last.

One day, just before the club started its western swing to Cincinnati, Chicago and St. Louis, Joe and Eddie found identical notes and railroad tickets in their mailboxes. They read: "You have been assigned to the Johnstown club in the Middle Atlantic League and are instructed to report there immediately."

Only then did the boys realize that the reason they had hung on so long was that the Middle Atlantic League season hadn't begun yet. It was a Class C loop, better than any league Joe had ever played in. However, his few weeks of exposure to the Pirates had steadied down the wide-eyed youngster who had left San Francisco, and he wasn't the least bit nervous. On the contrary, he quickly proved he was a fighter who exhibited no fear of anyone.

Soon after he joined the Johnstown team, he got into a

34

battle with an opposing player who didn't like the way Joe tagged him as he charged into second base, spikes high, while trying to steal. Punches were thrown and the next thing anyone knew the two were wrestling around in the dust and had to be separated by teammates.

After a few more incidents of this nature, opposing ball-players were more careful with Joe. "That Cronin's a tough kid," other managers warned them. "Don't tangle with him."

Umpires also found the young Irishman anything but an easy mark. One day, after he was called out at third base trying to stretch a double into a triple, Joe jumped to his feet and shoved his long jaw almost into the umpire's face, telling him exactly what he thought of the decision. Joe was thrown out of the game, but that didn't stop him. He continued to protest close calls that went against him.

He had a good year and so did the ball club. With Joe providing much of the spark, Johnstown won the Middle Atlantic League pennant. Barely one hundred and fifty pounds in weight and close to six feet in height, Joe looked gawky and frail, but he batted .313 and hit three home runs in his first year of organized baseball. And he enjoyed himself so much that he didn't even mind the small aggravations thrown into the team's path by the tightfisted owner of the club, who demanded a fee from his ballplayers for the use of their own clubhouse.

Joe and Eddie Montague dressed there once, then made other arrangements when they learned it was costing them money. Although the boys lived in a boardinghouse about three miles from the ball park, for the rest of the season they dressed in their room and hitchhiked in uniform to the games. By the time the season was over, they were so delighted to win the pennant that they left town with no rancor toward their inconsiderate boss.

In spite of his fine season, Joe realized that he hadn't

made much progress toward making the Pittsburgh ball club. The Pirates won the 1925 pennant under the shrewd direction of Bill McKechnie, and Glenn Wright was one of the stars in the victorious World Series. Joe could have batted .400 in Class C ball without making a dent in Pittsburgh's 1926 plans. Wright had the shortstop job nailed down so tightly that nobody could have pried it loose from him.

Back in San Francisco in the winter after the 1925 season, Joe continued to play ball wherever he could. On Sundays he collected ten dollars a game from the San Leandro semi-pro team in Alameda County, and twice a week he played for the Oakland Roofers. This team was owned by a young Arizona contractor named Del Webb, but Joe never laid eyes on the future New York Yankees owner that winter. They met and became close friends years later.

Between ball games, Joe worked for Philomena Hagar, who ran the San Francisco playground system. She was an ardent baseball fan, and Joe was one of her favorites. She sent him all over the city to organize ball clubs and umpire games, paying him by the day. Joe gave his mother everything he earned except his bare expenses.

"Just give me a few years," he told her, "and I'll buy you and Dad a new house."

Eddie Montague didn't go to spring training with the Pirates in 1926, and when Joe reported to Paso Robles he had a new roommate, a rookie outfielder named Fritz Brickell. The Pirates' outfield of Max Carey, Hazen Cuyler and Clyde Barnhart left Brickell with little chance to make the club, but, like Joe, he lived in hopes.

One day Joe remarked, "You know, Fritz, we'd be better off somewhere else. I can't beat out Wright and you'll never break into the outfield."

36

"You can learn a lot sitting on the bench," his roommate pointed out.

"I'd rather play in the minors than sit on the bench up here," Joe retorted.

He got his wish. Two weeks after the National League season began, he was farmed out to New Haven in the Class A Eastern League. There he met Billy Gleason, a second baseman who had had a couple of major league try-outs but had spent most of his career in the minors. Gleason taught Joe more about playing shortstop than anyone he had ever met before.

"You can make all the fancy plays in the world," Gleason told him, "but they don't do you any good if you boot the routine ones."

Day after day, before the rest of the team reported, he showed Joe how to handle his position properly. "You've got great hands, Joe," Gleason said. "I think you've got a good chance to make it."

"Against Glenn Wright?" Joe asked.

"He's not going to last forever."

"But he'll last too long for me," Joe said. "He's only twenty-five now."

"Don't get discouraged," Gleason said. "Just keep plugging and fighting. Something will happen when you least expect it."

One day in early July New Haven was losing a game in Springfield by three runs when Joe came up with the bases full in the ninth inning. Charley Reynolds, a good minor league hurler, was on the mound for Springfield. The count ran to two balls and two strikes when Joe began fouling the ball off. One after another, he spoiled the best pitches Reynolds fired at him. Disgusted, the veteran finally threw one across the heart of the plate. Joe, his bat cocked high, stepped into it and crashed it over the left field fence. He jogged around the bases behind his three teammates, reveling in the first grand slam home run of his professional career. When it proved to be the winning blow of the game, he confided to Billy Gleason in the locker room, "That was the greatest thrill of my life!"

"You'll have a million of 'em," Gleason assured him.

The Pirates recalled Joe in July, and once again he began having wild dreams of replacing the great Glenn Wright. But the Pittsburgh star was going strong, and Joe languished on the bench for weeks, watching the second base combination of Wright and Eddie Moore in action.

Then one day Wright was hurt sliding into second base. Joe pounded his glove and looked toward Bill McKechnie, just as the manager called, "Hal Rhyne!" Rhyne, ordinarily a second baseman, went in to play short and Joe continued to sit on the bench.

Soon after that, with Wright still out, Moore was taken out for a pinch hitter late in a game against the Cardinals at St. Louis. The batter drove in the tying run, and when the inning was over, McKechnie finally beckoned to Joe.

"Go in and play second, kid," the Pittsburgh manager said kindly.

Joe dashed out to a position he had never played in his life and happily fielded grounders thrown at him by George Grantham, the first baseman, before the game was resumed. He flipped the ball to Rhyne at short once or twice, hitched up his trousers and moved into position, trying hard not to be to conscious that he was in his first big league ball game.

The Pirates' pitcher had his troubles finding the plate, and the Cardinals got men on first and third with only one out and a right-handed hitter up. As Joe crouched to the right of second, two possibilities occurred to him. The man on third represented the winning run. If the ball were hit to him, Joe would have to make up his mind quickly whether to throw home or try for a double play.

If I throw home, there'll be only two out and two men on, he thought. But if I go for the double play, we'll be out of the inning.

The count moved to a strike and one ball, when the pitcher threw one on the outside corner of the plate. The batter reached out and sent a sharp grounder toward the hole between Joe and second base. He made a dive, barely grabbed the ball and, still on his back, tossed it to Rhyne, covering second base. His teammate whirled and threw to first and the Cardinals were out. The Pirates went on to win the game in the tenth.

Afterward Jewel Ens, the Pittsburgh infield coach, shook hands with Joe in the locker room. "Kid," he said, "that was a fine double play you started. What would you have done if the ball had been hit right at you?"

"I'd have still gone for the double play," Joe said.

"And not played safe by throwing home?"

Joe grinned. "Mr. Ens," he said without hesitation, "as long as I've got a fighting chance, I'll never play safe."

5.

BY THE TIME THE 1926 SEASON WAS OVER, JOE DECIDED THAT he needed more weight and strength if he expected to become a big league ballplayer. He was still painfully thin, and everyone who tried to help him told him the same thing, "Get bigger or you'll collapse if you have to play a full season."

He began drinking eggnogs and heavy cream between meals, and his mother gave him huge helpings of oatmeal and cream along with the rest of his breakfast. He walked four or five miles to the woods around South Street in San Francisco and spent hours chopping down trees. He oiled his bats to make them heavier and used them in semipro and pickup games. And he ran endlessly to strengthen his legs. When it was time to report to the Pirates for spring training in 1927, he had put on ten pounds and was in the best physical condition of his life.

He might just as well have stayed thin, as far as his chances of displacing Glenn Wright were concerned. Wright had had another great year in 1926, batting over .300 and retaining his place as the best shortstop in the National League. The Pirates had finished third, however, and Bill McKechnie's failure to win the pennant cost him his job. He moved to the Cardinals as a coach and was replaced by Donie Bush.

Joe expected to be sent to the minors again, but to his surprise Bush kept him with the Pirates. Joe sat on the bench for weeks, cooling his heels and fuming. Once in a while he got into a ball game, but he never played more than one inning at a time, and rarely had an opportunity to bat.

He threw his one big chance to make good out the window. Wright had to sit out a game and Joe started in his place at shortstop. With one out in the first inning, Joe made a fine stop of a hard-hit ball—then threw it over the first baseman's head. On the very next play, he made another great stop—and tossed the ball over the second baseman's head in an attempted double play.

After the inning was over, he trotted toward the dugout, arriving just in time to hear Jewel Ens say to Bush, "Gosh, we'd better get that kid out of there." Joe was back on the bench when the second inning began.

One day he came up as a pinch hitter and killed a rally in Chicago by hitting into a double play. Another time he faced Hub Pruett in Philadelphia and fanned on three straight pitches, trying to sock Pruett's soft stuff. Pruett had won fame in the American League for his ability to strike out the mighty Babe Ruth, so Joe knew he was in good company when he failed to hit the crafty veteran.

The Pirates moved into first place early in the year and stayed there all season. Joe continued sitting on the bench, feeling as if he were neither fish nor fowl. He was a member of the ball club, yet not a member, a man who wore a uniform but never got it dirty. He was sick and tired of getting

41

splinters on his pants. He hated the bench and would gladly have settled for a regular job with a last-place bush league team in preference to this job as a substitute on a major league pennant winner.

If it hadn't been for the friendship and loyalty of the club-house attendant, a youth named Socko McCarey, Joe might have asked to be sent back to the minors. McCarey, a Pittsburgh boy who knew he would never realize his life's ambition to be a big league ballplayer, transferred all his hopes to Joe Cronin.

"Joe," he said, day after day, "never get discouraged. You're going to be a great star someday."

McCarey didn't stop there. Early every morning he met Joe at Forbes Field and pitched to him for hours, while peanut vendors and groundskeepers and any other people who happened to be hanging around shagged the balls Joe hit. Both Joe and Socko were tireless, never satisfied no matter how long they practiced.

"Let's have some curves, Socko," Joe called one day. McCarey threw him curves all morning. "Fast balls today," Joe yelled another time, and fast balls were all he saw that day. McCarey threw him slow pitches, drops, inshoots, curves and fast balls every day for months. He pitched high and low, close and outside, over the plate and off center, while Joe stood swinging at the good ones and letting the bad go by.

Sometimes Joe said, "Socko, you're getting so good out there on that mound that you ought to give baseball another try."

"I'm not good enough, Joe," the other answered. "I just want to be able to show you what you might see when you get to be a regular."

"It might be a long time."

"Not as long as you think, Joe," Socko said. "Your chance will come. Just wait and see."

But the chance didn't come during that season of 1927. With Glenn Wright having another great year, the Pirates won the pennant going away. Joe played in twelve games, totaling exactly twelve innings. Except for the day he started and threw wild twice, he got in only as a relief for Wright in ninth innings. Even then, he never was sent into action unless the game were already won or lost.

He sat on the bench and watched the Pirates lose the World Series in four straight games to one of the greatest Yankee teams of all time. Paced by Babe Ruth, Lou Gehrig, Tony Lazzeri and Bob Meusel, the slugging New Yorkers toyed with the hapless Pirates. Joe didn't even appear as a pinch runner, and he felt like a thief when his series check arrived in the mail after he got home.

Nevertheless he continued to work hard, tried to put on more weight and build up his strength in any way he could. He had spent three years off and on with the Pirates and hadn't even come close to earning a regular job. Glenn Wright was still under thirty, and there seemed little hope for Joe in 1928, but he looked forward to the new season with eager anticipation.

One day he ran into Eddie Montague. After a couple of season in the minors, Montague was now with the Cleveland Indians.

"You've got a better chance than I have," Joe commented.

"Only because I got away from the Pirates," his old roomie confided. "I couldn't beat out Pie Traynor any more than you could beat out Glenn Wright."

"I wish they'd send me somewhere else," Joe said wistfully. "I'm getting sick of waiting for Wright to break a leg or something. Anyhow I wouldn't want him to. He's a great guy."

"Which doesn't do you one bit of good," Montague retorted. "But don't worry, kid. You're still young."

Considering his baseball experience, it was rather amazing just how young Joe still was. He had turned twenty-one on October 12, 1927, and would have been perfectly content except for one thing—he still wasn't playing regularly. His teammates were National League champions and had won two pennants in the years that Joe had known them. He had collected a full World Series share. He had been assured by experts that there was a great future in baseball for him, and, thanks to Socko McCarey, he was really learning how to hit.

But it was the same old story at Paso Robles in the spring of 1928. Joe, now weighing about one hundred and sixty-five, bigger, stronger and older, still couldn't compete with the great Glenn Wright. No matter how well he did in spring training, he knew he was headed for the bench—or the minors.

"I hope it's the minors," he told Joe Harris, a veteran outfielder who had been his roommate at Pittsburgh the year before. "At least I'll be able to play every day."

The Pirates broke camp and went to Los Angeles for some exhibition games before moving east. Every day when Joe asked for his mail at the Rosslyn Hotel, he hoped there would be some news of a change. Just before the team was due to leave for Pittsburgh, the desk clerk handed him an envelope with the words "Pittsburgh Pirates" in the upper left-hand corner. Joe ripped it open and read the note inside. Signed by manager Donie Bush, it said: "Your contract has been assigned to Kansas City." A railroad ticket was enclosed.

Joe didn't know whether to laugh or cry. True, he had been hoping for this, but now that it had happened he wasn't as happy as he had expected. Was this really what he wanted? Didn't it represent failure after a full year with the Pirates? And where would he go from Kansas City?

His doubts faded as he talked to Joe Harris. "It's a break, kid," Harris said. "Kansas City is Triple A—as close to the big leagues as you can get without actually being in them. And now you'll find out just how good you really are. They'll play you every day, and you'll be back up here before you know it."

It was a lonely trip east, and one of the longest Joe had ever taken by himself. When he arrived in Kansas City, he felt lost and a little sorry for himself. As he walked through the big Union Station carrying his battered old suitcase, he had twinges of nostalgia for San Francisco. The Excelsior playground would have looked good to him at that moment.

He felt better when he got to the ball park. The manager greeted him with open arms and assigned uniform number 17 to him. "It's a lucky one, Joe," he said. "It used to be Joe Hauser's."

Hauser, the minor league home run king, was with the Philadelphia Athletics after having had a big season the year before with the Kansas City Blues.

"I hope he left a few home runs in this shirt," Joe remarked as he tried it on.

"We'll soon find out," was the reply.

That afternoon the Blues played the Minneapolis Millers, and Joe, batting sixth, was the leadoff man in the second inning. The first pitch came in fat and tempting, and after a quick hitch at his pants, Joe belted it right out of the ball park. When he had crossed the plate, he jogged into the dugout with a big smile on his face and commented, "I guess Hauser didn't take all his home runs with him at that."

After such an auspicious beginning, Joe looked forward to fattening up his batting average at the expense of the

American Association pitchers. He had hit better than .300 both at Johnstown and New Haven and he saw no reason why he couldn't do as well at Kansas City. Somewhat to his surprise, the pitching seemed almost as good in Triple A ball as in the National League, and his average went down instead of up. After two months he was hitting around .240, and had added only one home run to his opening-day blast.

One day in Louisville, he remarked to his roommate Frank McGowan, "This is a tougher league than I thought."

"Nowhere near as tough as the majors," replied McGowan, who had spent two years with the Athletics. "If you can't hit here, you certainly won't do any better up there."

"What do you suppose is wrong?" Joe asked.

"Maybe you're not seeing the ball," the other suggested.

"I'm seeing it all right in the field," Joe said. "How can I be missing it at the plate?"

McGowan shrugged. "It happens, you know."

The more Joe thought about it, the more he wondered if McGowan were right. Each time he went to bat, he concentrated on watching the ball, trying to see it every split second as it approached the plate. Sure enough, he discovered that he often lost it just before he swung.

He talked the situation over with Chick Fraser, a Kansas City coach who also scouted for the Pirates.

"I'll tell you one thing," Fraser remarked, staring at Joe intently. "Your eyelashes are too long. I'll bet they get in the way. I'd cut 'em if I were you."

Joe cut them in the locker room that afternoon. His hitting didn't improve very much, but he did see the ball better. From then on, he clipped his lashes regularly.

His failure to hit bothered him more and more as the season progressed. McGowan was quite right—if he couldn't do well against American Association pitching, how could he expect to get anywhere in the big leagues? For that matter, how could he get back into the majors at all? Who would want a .240 hitter? A man would have to be an outstanding fielder to make up for an average like that.

However, Joe *was* an outstanding fielder. The Blues used him both at shortstop and third base, and he did well wherever he played. His ability to move in any direction, his quick reflexes and his powerful arm made him the talk of the league. Wherever he went, observers raved about the plays he made.

Just as at Johnstown and New Haven, the only other places where he had played regularly, Joe continued to be as scrappy a spark plug as ever. A "holler guy" and a natural leader, he needled his teammates, ragged his opponents and battled the umpires. He was in the midst of every argument, fighting over every close play that went against the Blues. He might have carried it a little too far at times, but this was only the result of his tremendous enthusiasm, his will to win. After watching Joe in action, more than one expert remarked, "This kid's worth having around if only for the trouble he makes."

In spite of his obvious love for the game and his refusal to give up, Joe was secretly beginning to get discouraged. Things weren't going too well with his father, so he sent home almost every cent he earned. He didn't eat properly, his clothes were a mess and he never spent money for pleasure. His financial troubles only added to his growing apprehension.

Despite his flaming ambition to become a baseball success, despite the assurance of others that his fielding and his fire might get him back into the majors, despite his own confidence that he would learn to hit eventually so that all the time Socko McCarey spent with him wouldn't be wasted, Joe was unhappy in Kansas City. Here he was—broke and a .245 hitter in Triple A ball. Furthermore, even if he added

47

a hundred points to his batting average, he saw no chance of ever making the Pittsburgh ball club. Glenn Wright was still going strong, still under thirty and still in Joe's way.

"Where can I go?" Joe asked Frank McGowan. "Who wants a kid like me?"

"You'll get a break," McGowan encouraged. "Just sit tight."

Waiting for what? Joe wondered. Perhaps, he thought, he ought to quit and go home to San Francisco. Philomena Hagar would always have a job for him in the playground system. Maybe that was the only thing he was good for anyhow.

One hot day in early August, after he had had a rough afternoon against mediocre Louisville pitching, Joe was getting ready to take a shower when Chick Fraser told him, "Go up to the front office after you're dressed. Joe Engel is there and wants to see you."

"Who's Joe Engel?" Joe asked.

"You'll find out when you meet him," was all the coach would say.

Joe dressed and showered, then headed for the front office. When he got there, a gray-haired man with a friendly grin introduced himself as Joe Engel. As the two shook hands Engel asked, "How would you like to change uniforms, kid?"

Joe sighed. "I'm hitting .245 and I know I'm due for a change all right. Where am I going—the Florida East Coast League or the Cotton States?"

"Neither. You're going to Washington."

Joe looked scornfully at the older man. "Look, mister," he said, "don't kid me. It's bad enough to be down and broke without having some guy take me for a ride."

"Maybe you're broke, but you're not down, son," Engel commented. "Get your baggage and come along."

"Are you serious, Mr. Engel?"

"I sure am, Joe. The Senators just bought you for seventy-five hundred dollars."

"Seventy-five hundred for a .245 hitter?" Joe repeated. "Are you out of your mind?"

"No, sir," the scout said. "I think you're worth every cent. That's why I told Clark Griffith to buy you. Now get your things and come along."

Joe stared, then muttered, "You really are serious, aren't you?" Jumping up, he exclaimed, "I'll be back in about two shakes, Mr. Engel."

As he started to leave, Engel stood up and followed him. "I'll go with you," he said. "We've got a train to make."

After Joe had picked up his meager belongings, Engel asked, "Where's your good suit?"

"This is it," Joe said.

"You can't go around in that. Take one of mine. We'll have it altered in Akron."

"Akron? I thought we were going to Washington."

"We are," Engel assured him. "Only I've got to finish up my scouting trip. I want to look at a pitcher in Akron and an outfielder in Youngstown. Then we'll head for Washington."

"Did you come all the way to Kansas City just to look at me?" Joe asked.

"As a matter of fact, I didn't. I came to look at a pitcher I heard about. But I forgot him when I saw you. I wired Griff yesterday and he told me to buy you today."

Joe wanted to ask what Engel had wired, but he didn't dare. Engel wouldn't have told him anyhow. The telegram read:

GRAB THIS KID CRONIN. HE DOESN'T LOOK LIKE
A HITTER, BUT HE SURE CAN FIELD.

49

The scout had sent another message back to Washington which he also kept to himself. This was a note to Griffith's pretty secretary Mildred Robertson, who also happened to be his niece. It said: "I'm bringing back a sweetie for you."

So, although Joe Cronin didn't know it, two members of the Griffith family were eagerly awaiting his arrival in Washington.

6.

Joe didn't impress either Clark Griffith or his niece when he shyly followed Joe Engel into the Senators' office in Washington. The suit Engel had given him had been hastily made over in Akron, but it still hung from his skinny frame like a tent. The waist was too roomy, the pants too long, the shoulders too wide. The hours on trains from Akron to Youngstown and from Youngstown to Washington, plus the summer heat, had left Joe exhausted and dirty, and since he had gone directly from the station to the ball park, he hadn't even had time to wash up.

"This is my new shortstop?" Griffith whispered to his scout. "You made me shell out seventy-five hundred dollars for him?"

"Wait until you see him on the field," Engel replied.

On the way out, Mildred stopped Engel and asked, "Him?"

When the scout nodded, she shook her head. "Maybe he'll turn out to be just my kind of guy," she murmured, "but he certainly doesn't look like much now."

But she liked the young Irishman from San Francisco

with the candid blue eyes and the square jaw, and she had a hunch she might like him even more in the future. However, she saw little of him that year. The season was nearly over, and Joe had no occasion to go into the office where she worked. The idea of asking her to go out with him never occurred to him. She was, after all, the boss's niece and Joe had no way of knowing that she might be interested in him. Besides, in his financial condition he couldn't afford to ask her for a date.

For lack of a solid infield, the 1928 Senators weren't going anywhere. They were in fourth place, with no hopes of climbing any further. Bucky Harris, the Senators' manager, was also the second baseman, although he was nearing the end of his playing days because of constantly recurring injuries. Dark-haired, gentlemanly son of a Pennsylvania coal miner, Harris had won everlasting fame as baseball's "boy manager" when, at the age of twenty-seven, he had led the Senators to their first pennant in 1924 and followed that with a spectacular victory over the New York Giants in the World Series.

Partly because Harris himself couldn't play regularly, Washington had been plagued by infield woes for a couple of years. Roger Peckinpaugh, a fine shortstop in 1924, slowed up badly in the next two seasons and was traded to Chicago. He had been replaced by Bobby Reeves, who had broken in as a third baseman but was converted into a shortstop in 1927. The experiment hadn't been a complete success, and it was still in progress when Joe joined the ball club in early August of 1928.

By September Harris was still experimenting, trying to find an infield combination that would give the ball club something to look forward to in 1929. Griffith wanted him to stick with Reeves at shortstop, but Harris was convinced Reeves would never make it. The Senators' manager, impressed with Joe Cronin's speed and spirit, intended to put the newcomer in at short a few days after his arrival, but Griffith objected. As a result, Joe stayed on the bench during much of the first long home stand, while Reeves remained in the line-up.

"Don't worry, Joe," Harris said. "You'll be in there soon enough. In the meantime, keep your eyes open and learn what you can about the American League."

The club went on the road right after Labor Day, with their first stop New York. The Yankees were one American League team that Joe knew something about. Ever since he had watched them wreck the Pirates in the previous World Series, he wondered how he would do against them. He got his chance to find out sooner than he expected.

Harris, plagued by a Charley horse, pulled up lame during infield practice. After limping off the field, he called Joe over and said, "Reeves will fill in at second for me and you're playing short. Go on out there and give it all you've got."

Less than a year before, Joe had sat in the visiting dugout and thrilled at the sight of the vast Yankee Stadium. Now he was playing in it himself. The Senators came up first, but they were out before Joe's turn came, since he was seventh in the batting order. When their half of the inning ended, Joe spat into his glove and dashed out to his position. He fielded the ball that Joe Judge threw him from first base in infield practice, tossed it back and forth to Reeves in mock double play maneuvers and took the throw from catcher Muddy Ruel after the pitcher was through warming up.

Then he settled down to play a ball game. Cedric Durst, the Yankees' leadoff man, sent a sharp grounder to his right, and Joe moved over, gracefully fielded it and threw the runner out by a couple of steps.

"Atta boy, Joe!" yelled Reeves beside him.

From then on, Yankee Stadium could have been the Excelsior playground, for Joe felt completely at home. Baseball was the same game in the "House that Ruth Built" as in the San Francisco sandlots. The only difference was in the caliber of the ballplayers.

Joe was completely relaxed when he came to bat against Tom Zachary with a man on first and one out in the second inning. He gave a hitch to his trousers as Zachary came out of his stretch, then smashed the first pitch between Durst in center and Bob Meusel in left. It rolled all the way to the fence, and by the time the ball was back in the infield, Joe was on third with a run-scoring triple.

Up again in the fourth, Joe sent home another run with a clean single that shot on a line over second base. Then, with a man on first and one out in the eighth, he hit one of Wilcy Moore's outside pitches along the first base line. It landed barely fair, slapping against the wall in deep right while Babe Ruth, playing Joe to pull toward left field, was forced to chase it almost from center field. It was another triple and a third run batted in for the kid from San Francisco.

The Senators won by a lopsided 11–0 score, and Bucky Harris didn't have to tell Joe to go back to shortstop for the second game. This time the opposing Yankee pitcher was Waite Hoyt, and Joe faced him for his first at-bat in the second inning. He took a called strike, then hit a sharp bounder which skidded between short and third for a single. When, three innings later, Joe sent a liner over short for another clean hit, he heard someone in the Yankee dugout growl, "That kid thinks he owns this joint."

There were two men on and two out when Joe came to bat in the seventh, with George Pipgras now hurling for the Yankees. Joe watched three pitches go by, setting the count at two balls and one strike, then swung at a fast ball.

It shot on a line between center and left, hit the front of the bull pen on one bounce and was good for three bases and two more runs batted in. The Senators won that game, 6–1.

"Well, kid," Bucky Harris remarked in the locker room, "looks like you've earned a job for yourself. Three triples and three singles your first time playing in Yankee Stadium is pretty good going."

After Joe thanked him, Harris added, "You're going to make it this time, Joe. And I'll play you as much as I can for the rest of the year."

The team went west and Joe remained in the line-up, even after Harris recovered from his pulled muscle. When the manager was ready to return to second base, the man who went to the bench was Reeves, not Cronin.

Joe didn't know it, but Harris received a telegram in St. Louis a week later from Clark Griffith. It read:

> KEEP REEVES IN THE LINE-UP. HE'LL NEVER
> BE A BALLPLAYER IF YOU DON'T.

Harris wasted no time answering his boss. "Neither will Cronin," he wired back. And Joe remained in the line-up until the season was over.

He finished with a .243 batting average, but he wasn't worried. The last thing that Harris said to him when he left Washington was, "You'll be a regular next year, Joe. You can't miss. Just put on a little more weight and you'll be as good a hitter as you are a fielder."

Now, for the first time in his life, Joe began to think that his dreams really might come true. The Senators needed him as badly as he needed them, and he made up his mind that he would be bigger and stronger, and a better hitter by 1929. He ate heavily and worked hard all winter, playing ball to keep his batting eye sharp but concentrating more on adding the weight he needed.

55

He suffered a short letdown in November when Bucky Harris left the Senators to manage the Detroit Tigers, but felt a thrill of anticipation when it was announced that Walter Johnson would replace him. Johnson had been a boyhood idol of Joe's, one of the greatest pitchers who ever lived, and a man with a reputation for being honest and fair minded.

"Do you think it will make much difference to you?" Joe's brother Ray asked.

"Not from what I've heard about Johnson," Joe replied. "If he thinks I'm good enough, he'll let me play."

Johnson didn't keep Joe in suspense very long. A month after spring training began in 1929 the new manager told him, "You're my shortstop, kid. When you learn to hit you'll be one of the best in this business."

With the help of a coach who was better known as a clown than a batting teacher, Joe was learning to hit. Al Schacht was famous as a funny man. He and Nick Altrock, another Washington coach, had teamed up on pregame shows which pulled fans in wherever the Senators went. The people who laughed at Schacht didn't realize that the former big league pitcher knew as much about baseball as anyone in the game.

Schacht had been attracted to Joe practically on sight. He liked the earnest youth whose whole life was devoted to becoming a ballplayer, and he made up his mind to help him as much as he could. Soon after Joe reported for spring training, Schacht said to him, "All you need to become a good hitter is practice. If you're willing to really work at it, I'll work with you."

"What do you want me to do, Al?" Joe asked.

"Come out to the ball park early in the morning and I'll pitch to you."

"That's easy," Joe said. "I did that in Pittsburgh."

"But I want you to work after games, too," Schacht told him. "And that's not so easy."

"Al," Joe said firmly, "as long as you're willing to pitch to me, I'm willing to swing a bat. I don't care if I drop doing it."

From then on, the two didn't miss a day. Joe stood at the plate for hours while Schacht threw him all manner of pitches. When the older man got tired, he found someone else to serve up the pitches while he stood behind the mound and watched Joe's every move at the plate.

"The big thing is to learn to hit the curve ball," Schacht told him. "Anyone can cream a fast ball. But the guy who can hit curves will never have to worry about being fooled too often."

Joe saw more curve balls in practice than he did in games that summer. Schacht showed him all the things a pitcher might do to hide his curve, all the ways a curve might go, all the tricks in a good hurler's bag. He went over every pitcher in the league, telling Joe who threw what and when, warning him what to look for in a given situation. Before the season was over, Joe had learned practically everything Schacht could teach him.

Although he didn't burn up the American League, Joe's hitting improved tremendously. He learned to wait for his pitch without leaving himself helpless if it didn't come. He watched for curves where he had once kept his eyes open only for fast balls. After a while, he could hit one pitch as well as the other.

"Don't be just a curve ball hitter," Schacht warned. "Remember, the fast ball will go farther when you hit it solidly. That's the pitch you want. But when pitchers find out you hit a curve just as well, they'll try to slip the fast one by you more often."

When the 1929 season ended, Joe had not only a respectable .282 average, but a reputation for being a potentially dangerous hitter. His eight home runs were hardly spectacular, but they showed that he had the power to belt a ball out of the park occasionally. And even though he led the league in errors, he was considered the best shortstop in the loop. Many of his misplays were on balls most shortstops wouldn't have reached. Some of the others were on throws which he tried to make from an unbalanced position after making a great stop.

It was a good season for Joe, but a disappointment for Washington fans, who had hoped that Walter Johnson, their beloved hero, would lead the team to a pennant. The Senators finished fifth, their first time out of the first division in seven years.

Still Clark Griffith was satisfied. "We're developing a good young infield," he told Johnson. "And we'll be all right in a couple of years."

He showed his satisfaction by giving Joe Cronin, the spark plug of the infield, a fat raise that winter. When Joe's contract arrived, it called for ten thousand dollars, the most money he had ever seen in his life.

He celebrated by making the down payment on a new house for his parents in the Balboa Terrace section of San Francisco.

7.

WHEN THE SENATORS REPORTED TO MANAGER WALTER JOHNson for spring training at Biloxi, Mississippi, in 1930, nobody expected miracles from them. They had a promising young second base combination in Joe Cronin and Buddy Myer, a rookie first base hopeful named Joe Kuhel, experienced veterans in the other positions and a pretty good pitching staff.

Except for Kuhel, this was fundamentally the same team that had finished fifth in 1929, and the experts thought that was just about where they would end up in 1930, especially since Kuhel obviously wasn't ready for the big leagues. But Joe Cronin disagreed violently with this consensus. Joe Judge, the veteran first baseman, still figured to have another good year left, and Cronin was convinced the Senators were being sadly underrated.

Before spring training was over, Joe remarked to Johnson, "You know, Barney, with half a break I think we could win the pennant this year."

"I'm glad to hear you say that, Joe," the manager replied.

59

"And if every man felt as you do, I'd be sure you were right."

Busy as he was on the field, Joe found himself eagerly looking forward to his dates with Mildred Robertson. Clark Griffith's dark-haired foster daughter and the tall, thin San Francisco Irishman had been attracted to each other from the moment Joe had first walked into the Senators' office in Washington two years before.

As her uncle's secretary, Mildred had been going south with the team for three years, but she and Joe didn't really begin going together until 1930, the first spring in Biloxi. Before the club broke camp, the two had become inseparable. When one was invited to a party, it was taken for granted that the other would be along. There were plenty of young married couples with the ball club, and the social life was active. Mildred and Joe soon found themselves in the middle of it.

At that point in his career, Joe could only dream of his future with Mildred. His older brothers were married and neither was making much money, so Joe had become the sole support of his aging parents. Marriage was definitely out of the question at the moment, but by the time the Senators returned to Washington for the start of the 1930 season, Joe knew that he would propose to her as soon as his finances permitted.

The season began with the Philadelphia Athletics, defending world champions, and the New York Yankees favored to battle it out for the pennant. Although Joe Cronin's spectacular shortstop play sparked the Washington Senators to a fine start, the Athletics went into a long early lead, and hopes for the pennant were quickly dashed. Even so, by May it was apparent that the Senators were a much better ball club than they had been the year before.

The reason was Joe Cronin. The promising young shortstop of 1929 was the outstanding star of 1930. He roamed all over the infield, making stops that defied the imagination, retiring base runners with quick, accurate snap throws, often from awkward positions. He was at his best when the chances were toughest and, oddly enough, at his worst when they were easiest. His only weakness was on ground balls hit directly at him, but with daily practice he continued to improve. What the fans remembered were his spectacular plays as he robbed opposing batters of what seemed to be certain hits.

One such play came in the second game of a doubleheader with the Boston Red Sox. With two out in the ninth and two men on base, Tom Oliver of the Red Sox lifted a high, twisting pop between third base and left field, which was sure to fall in for a single.

Joe was off with the crack of the bat, back-pedaling like mad and keeping his head up so that he wouldn't lose sight of the ball. While the crowd roared and Red Sox base runners dashed toward the plate, Joe seemed to lose any chance of catching the fly when he tripped and fell backward. As he was going down, he stretched as far as he could, and by some miracle the ball landed in his glove and stuck there. He landed heavily and rolled over once or twice in the grass, but he held on grimly and the ball game was over.

Thanks to his work with Al Schacht, his hitting was almost as spectacular as his fielding. In early May, he paced the Senators to a 13–5 victory over the St. Louis Browns, collecting two doubles and a triple off the combined slants of pitchers George Blaeholder and Sam Gray. That was the first of a long series of remarkable afternoons at the plate which found Joe's bat leading the Washington club to victories that kept it in the fight for second place.

Three weeks later Joe had a field day against Red Sox pitching in another doubleheader at Washington. He got a single which helped win the first game, 3–2, then really shelled the Boston hurlers with five straight hits in a 13–1 Senator victory in the nightcap.

"It's bad enough when he robs us of hits in the field," moaned manager Heinie Wagner of the Red Sox. "But when he kills us at the plate, too, it's even worse."

Joe not only "killed" the Red Sox, but others as well as the season progressed. In early July the inspired Senators began a drive to catch up with the first-place Athletics. This was the great Philadelphia team that had such stars as Lefty Grove, George Earnshaw, Jimmy Foxx, Mickey Cochrane and Al Simmons.

On the Fourth of July the Senators were in second place, three games behind the Athletics and a game and a half ahead of the third-place Yankees. With three victories in a row behind them, they moved into New York for a four-game series, beginning with the holiday doubleheader. Two veteran pitchers, Bump Hadley and Sam Jones, whipped the Yankees in this twin bill, but the star was Cronin. That day he did the job with his glove. Manager Bob Shawkey of the Yankees remarked later, "That Cronin is great. The only way to keep the ball away from him is to hit to the other side or into the air too far out for him to reach it."

The next day Joe's triple in the seventh inning set up the tying run for Washington and the Senators went on to win the game in the ninth. On July 6 he starred again in the field to help his team sweep the four-game series, and the Senators moved on to Boston one percentage point out of first place.

Joe's bat, comparatively quiet against the Yankees, caught fire in the series with the Red Sox. In the first game, he helped send the Senators into first place with three singles in four trips to the plate, and handled six tough chances without an error.

The next day Joe came up in the sixth inning with men

62

on second and third and one out—and the Senators behind, 5–4. He watched two called balls go by, then, realizing he wasn't going to see a good pitch, made up his mind to swing at anything he could reach. The next one was wide of the plate, but he stepped in and poked it into right field for a two-run single. Washington went on to win a 6–5 victory, their ninth in a row.

The following day they made it ten straight by winning the first game of a doubleheader, and, as usual, Joe starred afield and got a hit that set up a run. The Senators' streak ended as the Red Sox won the second game, but they were still in front of the pack.

By the middle of July the Athletics were back in first place, but the Senators were solidly entrenched in second and Joe, with a .315 average and sixty-six runs batted in, was their leading hitter.

He still had some great days left at the plate that season. One was July 23, when the Senators were in a slug fest against the St. Louis Browns. Behind by a run in the sixth, they moved out ahead when Joe belted a Sam Gray pitch into the left field bleachers with one man on and one out.

The next time he came up, in the eighth, Chad Kimsey was the St. Louis pitcher and the score was tied, 8–8. Joe watched a strike go by, then saw a curve ball exactly like the hundreds which Al Schacht had thrown at him during the endless practice sessions when Joe first joined the Senators. He timed it perfectly and again socked it into the seats in left field. That made it 9–8 and Washington finally won, 10–9. That was Joe's first two-homer day.

But his proudest performance of the season came on August 25 in Philadelphia, where the Senators faced the great Lefty Grove who was having one of his finest seasons.

The partisan Philadelphia crowd began heckling Joe the moment the game started. When he struck out in the first inning, their boos and catcalls grew louder, and every move Joe made after that was the signal for a chorus of bazoos. The Senators were behind, 2–0, when he came to bat with a man on first and two out in the fourth inning.

Grove, who rarely bothered to throw anything but fast balls in those days, whistled a strike past Joe, then moved him back with an inside pitch which was called a ball. Joe resumed his stance, nervously waving his bat across the plate, and leaning slightly forward. Grove stretched, glanced toward the runner and drove Joe back once again with another fast one high and inside. Now it was two balls and a strike, and Joe stepped defiantly back into the batter's box.

The big Philadelphia left-hander hardly bothered to look at first base. His stretch took only a split second, then he reared back and threw a blazing pitch right across the letters. Joe saw it coming and started his swing almost at the moment it left Grove's hand. Bat met ball with a crash, sending it toward the left field stands on a rising line.

It was hit so hard that Al Simmons, the Athletics left fielder, hardly moved from his tracks. He simply stood and watched the ball as it landed in the seats for a home run, tying the game 2–2.

The game remained tied until the eighth, when Joe came up again, this time with a man on second and one out. He took two fast balls, one for a strike, then Grove shaved him close again. With the count two balls and a strike, Joe figured the left-hander would have to get the ball over the plate. Grove poured it in and although Joe swung late, it went off on a line toward right field, dropping safely for a clean hit and sending the winning run home.

By September the Senators were solidly in second place, and they finished there. Walter Johnson's club had been the surprise team of baseball and Cronin the surprise player of the year. Joe led the shortstops with a .960 fielding average and with a healthy .346 batting average. He struck out only thirty-six times all year and stole seventeen bases.

When the season was over, *Spaulding's Guide*, then the official record book of the game, said, "In 1930, Cronin was the best young fielder in either league."

The Sporting News, the "bible" of baseball, went even further. In those days, the publication made the Most Valuable Player awards, which were then comparatively new. Al Simmons of the Athletics had received the first one, in 1929, and Simmons was a leading contender to repeat. Lou Gehrig of the Yankees, with a .379 batting average, and Lefty Grove were others expected to win the coveted prize.

To everyone's delight, the award went to Joe Cronin, who had practically hauled the Senators out of the second division by the bootstraps, with fifty-two out of a possible sixty-four votes.

Home in San Francisco, Joe spent the winter playing ball and corresponding with Mildred. When he reported back to Biloxi for spring training, he was that much nearer to marrying her, for Clark Griffith gave him a thousand-dollar salary raise. Joe was getting eleven thousand, which was good money in the depression year of 1931. Although it still wasn't quite enough for him to take on added responsibilities, Joe wasn't worried. He was only twenty-four—and still on his way up.

8.

In a way, Joe's great 1930 season did him more harm than good, for it put the burden of a 1931 pennant squarely on his slim shoulders. Not since 1924, when Bucky Harris had led the Senators to their first pennant, were Washington fans so excited about their beloved "Nats." If Joe Cronin, a year older and a year wiser, had another season like 1930, why shouldn't they win?

Why, indeed? The trouble with the fans' reasoning was that the Senators simply weren't that good. They had pitching problems which hadn't been solved. Manager Walter Johnson, admired and almost revered in his pitching days, wasn't cut out to be a manager. Everything had come so easy to him when he was playing that he couldn't understand why other players didn't do as well. The great "Big Train," one of baseball's gentlest souls under ordinary conditions, was testy and annoyed with anything less than perfection on the part of his ballplayers. He lacked the patience to run a ball club properly.

The fans made one other major mistake in their 1931

calculations. They forgot that Joe Cronin was still only a kid, as ballplayers go. In and out of the majors for six years, he had been a regular only for two. Furthermore, nobody knew whether he was really a .346 hitter or had batted well above his normal pace in 1930.

His hitting that year had given Joe confidence in himself, but he would have been the first to admit that he wasn't really that good. Even if he had been an experienced veteran, he knew he couldn't be expected to repeat that performance —and, in fact, he never did. Although he was a remarkable shortstop, an inspired player and hit a solid .300, he was not a .346 hitter.

He knew by the stories that were written and the way the fans talked that they expected him to carry the whole team on his shoulders. That was all right with Joe. He was used to responsibility; his parents had trained him well in that respect. And if the Senators failed to win and he didn't do as well as in 1930, he expected to take some of the blame.

He often talked the situation over with his roommate Heinie Manush, who had come to the Senators in the middle of the 1930 season in a deal with the St. Louis Browns. Manush also had something of a burden to carry, for the Senators had given up a popular outfielder named Goose Goslin for him and also pitcher Alvin Crowder. If Manush failed to fill Goslin's shoes, the fans would be on him, too.

"The only thing you can ever do is your best," Heinie told Joe. "If that isn't good enough, it's not your fault."

"I think we ought to win the pennant," Joe replied. "And if we don't, it'll be my fault."

"The heck it will, Joe," the other objected. "It takes nine men to make up a ball club."

The Senators, after a good start, didn't even come close. They were third, behind the Athletics and the Yankees by

67

early September. On the Sunday before Labor Day, thanks to Joe who hit for the cycle—a single, a double, a triple and a home run—they started a drive which brought them up to within two games of the second-place Yankees. Two weeks later, tied for second they went into Chicago for a series with the White Sox. They split the first two games and faced Tommy Thomas in the third.

Thomas was a good pitcher toiling for a poor ball club. In the first inning, Joe rapped a double which drove in a run. The White Sox tied up the game, and Joe came up again with two out and men on first and second in the fifth. He smacked the second pitch on a line between left field and center for another double and two more runs, but the White Sox again tied it up.

By the time Joe came up in the ninth, the veteran Red Faber, a spitball pitcher, was on the mound. There was one out, the bases were full and the score was tied at 5–5. Joe, who had become a fine curve ball hitter, had never been able to do much with spitters. The pitch had already been outlawed, but a few old-timers like Faber continued to use it.

Joe watched three of them go by, two for strikes and one for a ball. Then Faber, taking a full windup, threw another and Joe brought his bat around almost in slow motion, meeting the ball with a "squish." It floated on a soft line over the second baseman's head for a scratch single, just enough to drive in the winning run.

When the game was over, the Senators were in second place, but they couldn't stay there. Two days before the end of the season, they fell back into third, and that was where they finished.

The Washington fans were heartbroken. They wrote letters to the newspaper editors, blaming Cronin for the team's comparatively poor showing. Joe had hit .306, forty points below his 1930 mark, and that seemed to be all that mattered to the Senators' followers. They ignored the fact that he had driven in one hundred and twenty-six runs in 1931, matching his 1930 figure. They also overlooked other improvements, for Joe, while hitting only two less home runs, collected three more doubles and five more triples than he had the previous year.

Not everyone was against him. When the season ended, Frank Young, Washington *Post* baseball scribe, wrote the following concerning the fans' attitude:

"This is an injustice to one of the hardest-working and most conscientious players who ever wore baseball livery.

"Because Cronin hit .346 and was the Most Valuable Player last year, the fans expect him to do it all the time. They should forget about that .346 average. Irrespective of records, Joe Cronin is the outstanding shortstop in the majors. He'll be there when hits are needed, and he'll be fighting his heart out every day that he's able to walk."

Joe's own reaction to the criticism, when he read it at his home in San Francicso, was a shrug of resignation. "I did my best and it wasn't good enough," he told his father. "Next year maybe it will be."

He didn't get a raise for 1932, and he didn't expect one. When his contract arrived from Washington, he was glad to see that it didn't call for a cut. At least, he could hold his own in his dream to marry Mildred.

He still hadn't asked her, and didn't intend to until he was sure he could support a wife. They had a tacit understanding, but neither had put it into words. Mildred had obligations of her own, for she supported her mother, a responsibility she refused to give up, although Clark Griffith would have helped her. She could understand Joe's circumstances and was quite willing to wait for him.

Once again they corresponded all winter, looking forward

to a spring reunion in Biloxi. There they continued to travel with the baseball crowd of young married couples, confident that the time wasn't too far away when they might be married themselves.

The 1932 season began with a rush. The Senators opened in Philadelphia against an Athletics team which had just won its third straight pennant. Joe led off the third inning with a long home run over the right field wall, off Rube Walberg. In the fourth, after Sammy West tripled, Joe drove him home with a sacrifice fly. Joe collected two more singles before the day was over, and also robbed Mickey Cochrane of a sure hit with a great diving catch of a low line drive.

By late May, the Senators, Athletics, Yankees and Tigers were all battling for the league lead. On May 31 Washington moved within percentage points of the second-place Tigers, and Joe did his part. He came up in the ninth inning, with the bases empty, two out and the Senators trailing the Athletics, 3–2, and smashed pitcher Tony Freitas' first offering into the upper deck of the left field stands for the tying home run. The Senators went on to win in the twelfth inning.

The next day they went to Boston for a series with the weak Red Sox. They won both ends of a doubleheader, and again Joe helped, but the victories were costly both to him and the ball club. After he had clouted a homer and a single in the second game of the twin bill, he came to the plate against Ed (Bull) Durham, and was hit on the right thumb with a fast ball.

The pain was so intense that Joe fell to his knees, while Walter Johnson and the Senators' trainer Mike Martin rushed out to him. Martin took one look at the rapidly swelling thumb and said, "He'll have to come out, Barney. It may be broken."

The X rays didn't show a break, but the thumb was so badly sprained that he couldn't play for ten days. As he sat squirming on the bench during a western trip which found the Senators losing more games than they won, Johnson told reporters over and over, "We're dead without Cronin. We need his punch and we need his enthusiasm."

Day after day, the Washington manager asked Martin, "When can Joe go back?" And day after day, Martin answered, "Not yet, Barney, not yet."

Finally, just before a game in Cleveland, Joe went to the trainer and said, "Mike, my thumb doesn't hurt much at all any more. How about putting on a rubber bandage and letting me get back in there?"

"I hate to do it, Joe," Martin answered. "If you get hit there again, it might put you on the shelf for the season."

"I'm not going to get hit there again," Joe insisted. "Come on, Mike. Put on the bandage and let me get out there. The ball club needs me."

The trainer shrugged. "Okay," he agreed, "but for heaven's sake, be careful."

Joe was far from careful. He roamed all over the infield, making miraculous stops of hot shots and putting new fire into the team. He drove in one run with a single in the first inning, two more with a triple in the seventh. Thanks to him, the Senators won a lopsided victory.

For the first time in two weeks, Walter Johnson had a smile on his face as he talked to reporters in the hotel lobby that night.

"We're fifty per cent better with Joe Cronin back in the line-up," he said. "We can't get along with him out of there. Now that we have him again, I look for us to start winning consistently."

But the Senators didn't keep on winning, partly because they lacked the pitching, partly because Johnson couldn't mold them into champions. The immortal hurler of another era was just a so-so manager, still impatient because his pitchers couldn't pitch as he once had, still upset because the rest of the team failed to respond to his leadership.

In September Joe was hurt again by a pitched ball. This time, he suffered a split index finger on his right hand when Mel Harder of the Indians threw a curve ball too close to him. He insisted on remaining in the game, but he bruised a shoulder sliding into second base in the inning that followed, and Johnson took him out.

Joe was out for four days, and the Senators didn't win a ball game while he was gone. By the time Joe was ready to play again, the Senators were out of the pennant race.

They staggered through the rest of the schedule, with everyone but Cronin and Johnson lacking the incentive a pennant-winner needs. It was obvious that the old star was through as manager, especially since 1932 was the last season of a three-year contract which Griffith had given him at the end of the 1929 season.

Despite his injuries and disappointments, it had been a good year for Joe Cronin. He batted .318, a solid improvement over 1931, and had eighteen triples, the most of his career up to that time. While he hit only six home runs, almost every one of them was a clutch hit.

"Cronin," wrote a Washington writer just before the season ended, "didn't waste more than one home run this year. All the others either won games for the Nats or put them back into ball games which appeared to be lost."

The Senators finished third for the second straight year, with the Yankees and Athletics ahead of them in that order. Once again, they had failed in their quest for pennants that had eluded them ever since 1925.

9.

THE 1932 SEASON ENDED ON SUNDAY, SEPTEMBER 27, AND JOE had his tonsils removed the next day. He was out of the hospital within a week and was just getting ready to leave for home when Clark Griffith announced that Walter Johnson would not be retained as the Senators' manager for the 1933 season.

Griffith had never hired a manager from outside his own organization. George McBride, Clyde Milan, Ownie Bush, Bucky Harris and Walter Johnson, Griffith's previous managers, had all been promoted from the ranks. It was a foregone conclusion that Johnson's successor would be, too. The leading candidates seemed to be Sam Rice and Joe Judge, two smart old pros who had been with the ball club for years and whose playing days were practically over.

In common with everyone else who followed the fortunes of the Senators, Joe Cronin thought one of the older men would get the job. Both were close friends of his, and he knew he could get along with either. The idea that Griffith might have someone else in mind never occurred to him.

On the day before he planned to take the train for San Francisco, Griffith asked him to drop into the office before he left for home.

When Joe arrived, Griffith looked sharply at the younger man, then suddenly said, "Joe, I want you to manage the ball club."

"Me?" Joe exclaimed. "Why, Griff, I'm still a kid! I won't be twenty-six until next week."

"Well?"

"You mean you really want me?" Joe asked.

"Of course," Griffith replied. "If I didn't, I wouldn't offer you the job."

"Well, naturally I want it," Joe cried. "I'd be crazy if I didn't."

Griffith leaned forward in his chair and raised his hand. "Just a minute, Joe," he said quietly. "I wonder if you really understand what this job means. It's no bed of roses, you know. There are all kinds of problems that you're not likely to anticipate—not just problems of running the ball club, but other problems, too.

"You're a popular ballplayer—one of the most popular we've ever had in Washington. But the fans will be on your neck if you take this job. They'll second-guess you to death. They'll boo your brains out whenever you do something that doesn't meet with their approval. Most managers can stay in the dugout and let 'em boo, but you'll be out there where they can see you—get on you.

"They'll watch you on the field and they'll watch you off it," the old man went on. "You won't have a minute of privacy. Everywhere you go in this town, you'll run into baseball fans, and they'll buttonhole you and challenge you on every move you make.

"You'll have to be nice to newspapermen even after they've knocked your brains out. They'll ask you sharp

74

questions—sometimes impertinent ones—and you'll have to answer them in a way that will show them you're running the ball club—and what's more, do it without getting them sore. Sometimes you'll want to punch one of them in the nose, but if you do he can go a long way toward running you right out of Washington.

"And one more thing, Joe," Griffith added. "What you did yesterday doesn't mean a thing. All that counts is what you do today. Bucky Harris was booed out of town three years after he won his second straight pennant. In 1924 and 1925 everyone here from President Coolidge on down thought he was great. By 1928 the fans were murdering him."

Griffith leaned back, spread his hands wide, held Joe's eyes in a steady gaze and asked, "Do you still want the job?"

"Griff," Joe said, "you haven't told me a thing I didn't know. I still want the job."

"Okay, son," Griffith agreed. "It's yours."

The announcement of Cronin's appointment was made on October 8, 1932, four days before his twenty-sixth birthday. When Griffith assembled the newspapermen in his office to present the new Senators' manager, he said, "I picked Cronin because baseball is the big thing in his life. He thinks baseball all the time. He's smart—and he's a fighter. I think he's going to make a great manager."

A Washington columnist's answer to that the next day was "Why ruin a great shortstop to make a doubtful manager?" In general, however, the Washington sports press hailed the surprise selection. Everyone who knew Joe, or had seen him in action, admired him, while the fans obviously were more than ready to give him a chance.

When somebody asked Cronin if he expected to lead the Senators to a 1933 pennant, he replied, "I'll certainly try. But all a manager can do is keep the players hustling. Anyone who reaches the big leagues knows what it's all about. A manager can't play for him. The manager's big job is to keep the boys on their toes, and that's what I intend to do."

"He'll put life and spirit into the ball club," penned a Washington writer the next day. "And that's what it needs more than anything else."

The Senators needed more, much more, and nobody knew that better than Joe. On his last day in Washington before going home, he said to Griffith, "We've got to get pitching help—left-handers particularly."

"I have a few in mind," Griffith remarked. "We'll see what we can do at the meetings."

"The Tigers have Earl Whitehill on the block," Joe said. "He can beat the Yankees. So can Walter Stewart, if we can get him from the Browns."

"I'd like to get Goslin back, too," Griffith added.

Joe took Mildred out that night, and as he looked at her across the dinner table he wished he could ask her to marry him that very minute. But first he wanted to make sure that his parents would be taken care of for the rest of their lives. Furthermore, he didn't intend to let anything get his mind off his job. His whole future depended on the 1933 season. If he did well, he could think about marriage then. In the meantime, since he and Mildred had waited this long, they could wait a little longer.

Joe spent the next two months keeping in shape as he always had, and talking at length by telephone to Clark Griffith. For the first time in his life, Joe was going to the December baseball meetings, which were held in New York that year. He left by train for Washington on the sixth, and after a couple of days there, he went to New York with his boss.

The winter meetings were always a hail-fellow-well-met,

back-slapping gathering of the baseball clans. Owners, managers, newspapermen, people looking for jobs and general hangers-on congregated in the lobby or in hotel suites and talked shop. Ostensibly, the meetings were to discuss problems and pass on various proposals, but actually they were used as the medium for making player deals. In those days there were more trades made during the winter meetings than at any other time of the year.

Joe divided his time between the lobby of the Hotel Commodore and the suite he shared with Clark Griffith. He enjoyed the meetings and the chance to shake hands with old friends and new, but his principal interest was in how much luck the Senators might have in getting the men they needed.

They went to market with several good ballplayers for bait. They could spare Firpo Marberry, a relief pitcher, if they got one or two of the hurlers they were after. Joe Kuhel was going to be the Senators' first baseman for a long time to come, but they had a fine-looking young rookie first baseman named Harley Boss, in whom several teams had shown more than passing interest. They were also willing to give up Sam West, a top-ranking outfielder, and Lloyd Brown, a front-line pitcher.

Joe was especially eager to land Stewart and Whitehill, and he agreed that Griffith should do everything possible to get Goslin back into a Washington uniform. As it turned out, the Senators' executives, one of the oldest and the very youngest at the meetings, were among the few who knew exactly what they wanted and exactly what they could afford to sacrifice in order to get it.

They made their first deal on December 14. After dickering most of the night with the St. Louis Browns, the Senators gave them West, Brown and a chunk of cash for

77

Stewart and Goslin. The next morning they completed a trade with the Tigers, handing them Marberry and Carl Fischer for Earl Whitehill.

"We're doing all right, Griff," Joe commented. "We've got the two left-handers we wanted, plus Goslin. But we've given up a lot of relief pitching strength. I'd like to get somebody else for the bull pen."

"Cleveland is talking about Boss," Griffith replied. "I think they'll give up Jack Russell for him, but I'll want somebody to play first base for our farm club."

"Russell would be fine," Joe nodded.

The next day the Senators got Russell and a veteran minor league first baseman named Bruce Connatser for Harley Boss, and that was the last deal they made at the meetings. Griffith, "the Old Fox," and Cronin, the young one, left New York with everyone they had sought, and they hadn't been forced to give up a single man they couldn't spare.

Back in Washington, Cronin tried hard to be conservative when talking to newspapermen about the deals, but he found it hard to hide his elation. Publicly he announced, "I think we've helped our ball club with these deals." Privately, he and Griffith agreed that, barring accident or injury to a key man or two, the Senators had the man power to win the 1933 pennant.

"You got me the men I asked for, Griff," Cronin said. "Now it's all up to me."

"Don't be too optimistic, Joe," the old man cautioned. "Remember, there are one hundred and fifty-four games in the schedule and something that could hurt you might happen in any one of them."

Joe went home with line-ups and batting orders whirling around in his head. He would pore over the personnel on the ball club for the next three months until he knew exactly how to handle the men by the time the season began.

In the meantime, in discussing the winter meetings, newspapers around the country were speculating on the trades that had been made there. Practically everyone agreed that the Senators had the best of every deal they made, but nobody knew whether they were Cronin's deals or Griffith's. Knowing Griffith's reputation for shrewdness, it was conceded that the old man must have done most of the thinking. Actually, Joe had been the one who asked for most of the pitchers they got, but this wasn't generally known.

Babe Ruth, who was nearing the end of his glorious playing career, was asked what he thought about Cronin as a potential manager during an interview in January of 1933. "Cronin," the Babe remarked, "is too young to manage and play, too. He ought to stick to his shortstop job and let somebody else run the ball club."

When this was called to Joe's attention in San Francisco, he laughed and said, "Babe Ruth is entitled to his own opinion, just the same as any bleacher fan. I think I'll get along all right."

A day or so later, Griffith told Joe the Senators had a chance to get Luke Sewell, veteran Cleveland catcher.

"Grab him, Griff," Joe said. "He's a solid receiver and a pretty good hitter."

So Griffith sent cash and Roy Spencer, who had done the bulk of the Senators' catching in 1932, to the Indians for Sewell, completing what must have been one of the most astute series of player deals ever made. The Senators had strengthened their pitching, their catching and their outfield. If everyone remained healthy, they indeed had a fine chance to win the 1933 pennant.

In February Joe left home for spring training at Biloxi with a song in his heart, for he was certain that he could

79

become the youngest manager of all time ever to lead a team to a major league championship.

"If I don't," he told Mildred, "it won't be for lack of man power."

"Or effort," she added.

"That," Joe commented, "goes without saying."

10.

Rarely in major league baseball history has one man dominated a season as Joe Cronin did in 1933. As the youngest big league manager of all time, he was a source of nationwide curiosity and interest from the moment his appointment was announced. When the square-jawed twenty-six-year-old Irishman, known wherever baseball was played as "Frisco Joe," met his ball club for spring training, he found himself under a blinding spotlight which might have turned the head of many another young man.

Joe was well aware that he was living in a goldfish bowl. He knew that he was on a spot which called for almost instantaneous success. He couldn't afford to do anything wrong, for it would mean not only his own downfall but would place Clark Griffith, whom he loved almost as much as his own father, in a painfully embarrassing position.

He had read the stories about himself, and knew that more than one baseball expert around the country was referring to his appointment as "Griffith's Folly." He knew, too, that Walter Johnson was still immensely popular with the fans, and he would have to prove his right to replace the immortal veteran. This meant only one thing—Joe had to win a pennant.

Despite Johnson's failures, Cronin had the highest regard and respect for his former manager who now managed the Cleveland Indians. One of the first things he had done after being named Johnson's successor was to pick up the telephone and say, "Barney, I want you to know that Griff offered me the job." And Johnson had answered, "Joe, there's nobody who deserves it more."

When Cronin arrived in Biloxi, he knew he couldn't waste a day in trying to transform the Senators from lackadaisical athletes, satisfied to have finished third in 1932, into a fighting, inspired unit of men who would settle for nothing less than first in 1933.

On the day practice began, Joe stood in front of his men and said, "I don't intend to finish lower than the top. We're going to win the pennant. No matter what happens, just remember that. We're the best team in baseball, and we're going to prove it."

That night he sat around the hotel lobby talking baseball. When he went to bed it was not in a suite as other managers did, but in a room exactly like those occupied by his ballplayers. The next day he ran around the field with everyone else, got into the good-natured kidding sessions that are characteristic of all ballplayers, slapped men on the back, grinned and swapped wisecracks with them and showed that he was no less one of the boys than he had ever been.

It wasn't long before his men responded. Before the end of the week, one veteran who had been openly skeptical before spring training began, said, "I thought this kid was going to go high-hat, but he isn't. If there's anything I can do to help him, I'm going to do it."

Within two weeks the Washington Senators were behind Joe Cronin as they had never been before. They loved this kid who was not only their boss but their friend, who refused to concede that there was a team in baseball better than his own, who insisted that the Senators were going to win the pennant long before the race had even started, who made everyone work hard but didn't let up on himself, who lived as they lived, traveled as they traveled and played as they played.

As the weeks progressed, they began to marvel at Joe's perceptiveness and understanding. He seemed to know instinctively how to handle each individual. He was genuinely interested in their problems and wanted them to be contented and happy. If a man was worried about illness in the family, Joe told him, "Take some time off—as much as you need." If there were financial problems, he tried to help. Soon the word got around that this youngster was a person who could be confided in, and veterans and rookies alike went to him with their troubles.

Joe had a weakness at that time which remained with him all his life—he hated to fire anybody. When cut-down time came, he had to fight with himself to tell men they had to be dropped. He never did it bluntly or coldly; instead, he always said something like, "You'll be back" or "Don't let it get you down." Even the men who received such bad news left with feelings of warmth and good will toward him.

The team broke camp in early April and barnstormed home to Washington for opening day against the Philadelphia Athletics. Manager Connie Mack had already begun to break up his great team. He had sold Al Simmons and Jimmie Dykes to the White Sox, the first of a series of moves which eventually would find all of his great stars on other teams. The Athletics had failed to win the pennant

83

in 1932, after taking three in a row, but they were still dangerous. Joe wanted desperately to get off on the right foot by beating them in the opening game of the season.

A distinguished crowd, including President Franklin D. Roosevelt, was on hand for the first game of the season. When Griffith introduced Joe to the new president, it was one of the thrills of his life. He stood by and watched F.D.R. throw out the first ball, accepted his good wishes with a handshake and then, for the first time in his life, presented his own starting line-up to the umpire. It included Joe Kuhel, Buddy Myer, Joe Cronin and Ossie Bluege in the infield, Heinie Manush, Goose Goslin and Fred Schulte in the outfield, Luke Sewell behind the bat and Alvin Crowder on the mound. Except for the pitcher, this was the team which would be playing for him during most of the season.

Tony Freitas was the starting pitcher for Philadelphia. He got the first three Senators in order, but Joe led off the second inning with a single. Goslin drove him home with a two-bagger for the first run of the game, and the Senators, with Joe collecting two more hits, won an easy 4–1 victory. By the time the game was over, the crowd was in an uproar, and even the President didn't leave until the last man was out.

It was the good start that Joe had wanted, but there were still one hundred and fifty-three games to go and each could provide its own special obstacle. The Senators spent the next two weeks floundering around, losing almost as many games as they won and looking like anything but potential pennant-winners, while the Yankees, defending champions, took over the league lead almost at once.

Joe blamed himself for the Senators' poor showing, for he was in a dreary batting slump which also affected his fielding. His batting average hovered around .240, and he transformed easy plays into costly errors. But he never stopped fighting as he goaded his mates and gave himself pep talks in private.

The ball club needed a push from the outside, the kind that even an inspirational young leader like Joe couldn't provide. The push came during a short series with the Yankees at Griffith Stadium in the last week of April. Riding high, the Yanks murdered the Senators in the first of two games. Halfway through it, Ben Chapman, the leading base stealer of the American League, slid into second base and ripped Buddy Myer's stocking to shreds. The two had words, for this sort of thing had happened before, but no blows were struck.

The next day, with the Yankees ahead by a run in the fourth inning, Tony Lazzeri came to bat. One man was out and Chapman on first base when Lazzeri sent a hot shot to short. It was an easy double-play ball; Joe quickly fielded it and tossed it to Myer, covering second. Chapman, out by several feet, came in with his spikes high. As Myer jumped to avoid him while trying to get the ball away, the Yankee base runner slashed Myer's foot with his spikes. The Washington second baseman, unable to throw and boiling mad, kicked the prone Chapman, who jumped up and grabbed Myer. While the two wrestled around, Joe, followed by members of both teams and the umpires, rushed over to separate them.

During the next five minutes, both Joe and the Yankee manager, Joe McCarthy, argued with the umpires that the man on the other team should be banished from the game. The men in blue finally settled the issue by throwing both players out. The Yankees could spare Chapman more easily than the Senators could Myer, and Cronin protested so violently that he almost got himself exiled. He quieted down only when threatened with expulsion, then told

85

Johnny Kerr to play second base and started back to his own shortstop position.

But the affair wasn't quite over. In order to get to the Yankee locker room, Chapman had to walk through a runway beside the Senators' dugout. As he approached the bench, the Washington ballplayers yelled insults at him, and when he started down the runway steps, Earl Whitehill reached out and grabbed him. Chapman promptly belted Whitehill in the face, starting another fight.

Once again Joe rushed over to help break it up. He took a look at Whitehill, and for a moment thought he saw all his hopes being washed away in the blood on the pitcher's slashed lips. Angry all over again, Joe turned toward one of the umpires and demanded action. The only action that came was the banishment of Whitehill for instigating the rumpus.

By this time Joe was fit to be tied, and several of his mates grabbed him to prevent his getting thrown out, too. The mess was unraveled at last and Joe, still in the ball game but so angry he could hardly concentrate, finally returned to his post. For the moment, the Senators fell apart, and the Yankees belted out a 16–0 victory. The next day it was announced that Whitehill, Myer and Chapman were all suspended for three games. Whitehill, as it turned out, was not badly hurt. He was able to pitch as soon as his suspension was lifted.

The Senators still struggled for another week, but the fights in Washington had fused them into the one-for-all, all-for-one unit that Joe had been trying to build. They lost a few more ball games, but then started climbing, and by mid-May were tied for second place, four games behind the league-leading Yankees.

Then Joe suddenly caught fire, inspiring the whole team. On May 16 he drove in the winning run as the Senators beat the Indians in the twelfth inning. The next day, he had two singles and two doubles in four trips and led the Senators to another victory over Cleveland. On through the home stand Joe continued to hit like mad. When it was time for the ball club to take to the road, he had raised his average from .246 to .320. During that period Joe had thirty-three hits in seventy-four times at bat for an astounding .446 mark.

Cronin and his ball club were just beginning their drive, however. They left Washington a game and a half behind New York, on a sixteen-game jaunt through the East and West. With Joe leading the way, they took three out of four in St. Louis, four straight in Chicago, two out of three in Detroit, three in a row in Cleveland.

Everybody belted the ball, but Joe's hitting was fantastic. On June 19 he got five hits in six times up, on succeeding days four out of five and four out of four. In the sixteen games he had thirty-five hits in sixty-eight trips to the plate, an unbelievable .515 pace, boosting his average to .344. The Senators won thirteen of those games, and when they arrived home, every regular except Buddy Myer and Luke Sewell was hitting over .300.

They finally caught the Yankees on June 23 and passed them the next day. By the end of June, only half a game separated the two clubs, and it was apparent that the Fourth of July doubleheader at Yankee Stadium would go a long way toward settling the pennant race. When the Washington ball club moved into New York for this payoff twin bill, over seventy-seven thousand fans were in the stands to watch it.

In the first inning Manush doubled and Cronin drove him home with a single. The game rocked back and forth as first one team scored, then the other. By the last of the ninth it was tied up at 5–5.

Manush was the leadoff man in the tenth, with Cronin following. As the two stood near the on-deck circle, Heinie said, "Joe, if I double again, will you drive me in the way you did in the first?"

"It worked once," Joe replied. "Maybe it will again."

Sure enough, Manush belted the second pitch to right center for two bases. And sure enough, Joe smashed the first offering to him on a line to dead center, driving his teammate home with the winning run.

Walter Stewart pitched the second game for Washington. Joe collected one hit, a triple, but died on third base. However, his inspired ball club piled up three runs while the desperate Yankees could nick Stewart for only two. The sweep of the twin bill sent the Senators home two and a half games in front of the pack.

The team returned to Washington without their manager, for Joe had been selected as the American League shortstop for the first major league All-Star game, which was being played in Chicago. He traveled with Crowder, Babe Ruth, Lou Gehrig, Tony Lazzeri, Ben Chapman and coach Art Fletcher of the Yankees, all of whom had been chosen. When Ruth saw Cronin on the train, he grinned and said, "There's Mr. Big."

"For now anyhow," Joe grinned back.

And at that halfway point of the season, he was indeed "Mr. Big." With a glittering .362 average, he was leading the league in batting, and his team was at the top of the American League pennant race.

11.

WHEN JOE RETURNED TO WASHINGTON FROM THE ALL-STAR game, there were several hundred people at the railroad station to greet him. His teammates had already been given a big welcome after sweeping the Yankee doubleheader in New York, and the fans had missed him. Now they cheered and whistled as he got off the train, and he needed a police escort to reach his car, where Mildred was waiting for him.

"Just imagine, Mil," he exclaimed as they drove away, "all those people taking the trouble to come down just to see me. And with the season only half over, we haven't really done anything yet."

"Everybody's sure you will, Joe," she assured him. "The whole town's positive the Senators will win the pennant."

"I hope the whole town's right," he said. "We're going to need plenty of luck. If a key man gets hurt, it could kill us."

Three days later he thought it had happened. The Senators were playing the White Sox at Griffith Stadium when Joe came to bat in the fifth inning. The Chicago pitcher

89

was Chad Kimsey, a fast ball specialist who had once been with St. Louis. He crossed Joe up with a change-up for a strike on the first pitch, then, as Joe leaned in close to the plate, he threw one high and hard.

Ordinarily Joe would have moved back a step and let the ball go by him, but this time, for some inexplicable reason, he froze. His feet seemed anchored, his body immobile as the flying pellet came toward him, and he knew he was going to be hit. At the last minute, he managed to shield his face with his arm and the ball caught him squarely on the left elbow.

Gasping with pain, Joe went down. As Mike Martin, the Senators' trainer, and Al Schacht, the third base coach, ran out to him, Schacht whispered, "Not Joe—not Joe—anybody else—but not Joe—"

When at last Martin could look at the elbow, Schacht asked, "Is it broken?"

"I don't know," the trainer replied. "He'll have to go for X rays."

Joe was finally able to sit up. With a wry grin he exclaimed, "Wow, did that hurt!"

With Martin and Schacht helping him, he gingerly got to his feet and walked to the dugout under his own power. The last thing he did before heading for the locker room with the trainer beside him was to tell Schacht, "Move Buddy Myer to short and put Johnny Kerr on second, Al. You're in charge until tomorrow. That's when I'll be back."

"I sure hope you're right, Joe," the other said.

Joe's arm wasn't broken, but it was bruised badly enough to keep him out of uniform for a couple of days. Dressed in street clothes and with his arm in a sling, he ran the team from the bench. The Senators missed his punch, and barely broke even, winning three of the six games they played without him.

Anxious as he was to return to short, Joe found one compensation in sitting on the bench—he could concentrate on running the ball club. Later he told Schacht, "Someday I might enjoy being a bench manager. You can do more from there than you can from the field."

"I'd rather see you on the field," Schacht said. "When you're old and gray, you can manage from the bench all you want."

Joe's hitting fell off when he returned to the line-up, but he had expected that. In the meantime, he continued to come through with clutch hits. By the end of July, the Senators were three and a half games ahead of the second-place Yankees. They still held that margin when they went into Yankee Stadium for a five-game series on August 7.

To the horror of their faithful fans back home in Washington, the Senators dropped a doubleheader that day. Now they were only a game and a half ahead, and could conceivably leave New York in second place, if the Yankees swept the remaining three games.

Joe called the team together in the locker room just before the third game of the series.

"Boys," he said quietly, "we are going to win the pennant." He looked at the circle of faces around him. "Do you understand that? *We're going to win.* We had a bad day yesterday and we'll have more bad days before this race is over. But no matter what happens, remember—we're going to win the pennant. We start today."

And behind Walter Stewart's fine pitching, they whipped the Yankees that afternoon. They did it again the next day behind Al Thomas, and they did it a third time behind Earl Whitehill. That put them a game further ahead of the Yankees than they had been when they came to town.

The Senators were never again in danger. After they had swept a four-game series in Chicago in mid-August, Shirley

Povich, the able sports columnist of the Washington *Post* wrote:

"Some people call it ambition. Others call it inspiration. But the correct word is hustle. That's what Cronin has imparted to his ball club, and his players are almost perfect counterparts of the dashing young leader, who is a highly concentrated bundle of energy out there on the field."

With his team far ahead of the pack in early September, Joe went into a short batting slump. He couldn't buy a hit for several days. Finally one afternoon in Philadelphia he said to Al Schacht, "If I go for the collar today, how about pitching to me after the game?"

Joe failed to get a hit that day, so Schacht rounded up bat boys and other youngsters who came to watch their idols in batting practice, stationed them around the field and spent half an hour pitching to Cronin. While the delighted kids happily shagged flies for him, Joe was able to regain his batting eye.

Three days later, the Senators whipped the Yankees two days in a row, Joe winning both games with clutch hits in the late innings. After the second contest, Heinie Manush, who was batting .332 to Joe's .315, declared, "That Cronin is the greatest money hitter in baseball."

They clinched the pennant on September 21 by beating the St. Louis Browns before a ladies' day crowd that almost filled Griffith Stadium to capacity. The last out was made by Manush on a fine catch of Oscar Melillo's long fly ball. As soon as Heinie grabbed it, Joe jumped high in the air, then began trotting toward the dugout, shaking hands with one ballplayer after another as he went on his way.

Suddenly he was aware of a shrieking mob of happy women pouring out of the stands and rushing toward him. Without a moment's delay, Joe sprinted for the runway and barely got inside before the first of the ladies reached the dugout. He stayed in the locker room for nearly two hours, accepting and handing out congratulations. Then, shaved, showered and dressed, he started out the door.

"Better not go out that way, Joe," somebody said. "You won't get ten feet. There must be a thousand women out there."

"Still there, eh?" Joe said grinning. "I hate to disappoint them all."

"Disappoint them?" repeated a baseball writer. "Do you want to get killed?"

"Maybe I'd better go out through the field at that," Joe agreed.

He went back through the runway and up the steps to the field, intending to go out a side entrance. But the moment he started walking toward it, he realized he would never make it there either, for a howling mob of women was already beginning to pour out of the stands.

I've got to run for it, he thought. Then he sprinted for the fence, where he knew a trap door led to the street, as the feminine fans followed like hounds chasing a fox. He barely won the weird race, and it was months before he heard the last of it from those who saw his mad escape from the exuberant ladies.

Joe Cronin was the most talked-about figure in baseball for the next two weeks. His name appeared in headlines on sports pages all over the country, as feature writers swamped him for interviews. Even the fact that Bill Terry, another player-manager serving his first full year in that capacity, led the New York Giants to a National League pennant failed to detract from Joe's luster. Terry was older than Joe and nowhere near as attractive a personality. The veteran first baseman, who had succeeded John McGraw as the Giants' manager in mid-season of 1932, was a cold, rather grouchy man who had no patience with newspapermen and was already feuding with them.

This was Joe's opponent in the World Series coming up. Because he was popular and Terry was not, the Senators were sentimental favorites to win the Series. Joe wanted desperately to cap the greatest season of his life with a world's championship, but the Giants were tough, and he knew it.

Furthermore, they had gained inspiration from their own shortstop Blondy Ryan. Ryan, temporarily out with an injury, had wired Terry just before taking the train west to join the team, "They can't beat us." Terry put the telegram on the locker room bulletin board, and later took it with him all around the circuit. He pointed to it at every opportunity, and it gave a lift to the whole team.

The first game of the Series was at the Polo Grounds in New York on October 3. Joe debated until almost the last minute about whom to start on the mound. Crowder had won twenty-four games, but he was a right-hander and the Giants had several long-hitting left-handed batters, including Mel Ott, Joe Moore and Terry himself. Joe finally nominated the left-handed Walter Stewart to face the great Giants' southpaw Carl Hubbell.

Mel Ott whacked a home run with a man on base in the first inning, and the Giants scored two more in the fourth. That was all Hubbell needed despite two hits by Joe, one of which drove in a run for the Senators. The Giants ace fanned ten Washington batters, and, except for Joe, only Schulte and Myer could hit him, Schulte getting two singles. The Giants won that one, 4–2.

Alvin Crowder faced Hal Schumacher in the second game, which was close for a while. Goslin belted a home run in the third to put the Senators in front, but Crowder, after shutting out the Giants for five innings, suddenly fell

94

apart in the sixth. When the inning was over, the Giants had piled up six runs. They won, 6–1, giving them a two-game lead in the Series.

The clubs moved on to Washington, where President Roosevelt threw out the first ball before a sellout crowd. Earl Whitehill was the Senators' hurler, while Freddy Fitzsimmons pitched for New York. Before the game began, Cronin told Whitehill, "It's all up to you. We can't afford to lose this one."

"Just get me a fast run or two," the left-hander replied, "and I'll hold 'em."

The Senators got him three runs in the first two innings and, true to his promise, Whitehill handcuffed the Giants, shutting them out with a glittering five-hitter. Washington's ultimate 4–0 victory put them right back in the Series again.

Joe happily wandered all over the locker room after the game, patting regulars and substitutes alike on the back and swapping wisecracks.

"They're only a game ahead of us now," Joe yelled. "Tomorrow we tie it up."

It was Hubbell's turn to pitch again for the Giants, and Joe sent Monte Weaver against him. The two put on a magnificent pitching duel. Terry belted a homer in the fourth, but the Senators tied up the game in the seventh on Joe Kuhel's single, Ossie Bluege's sacrifice and a hit by Luke Sewell. That finished the scoring for the regulation distance, and the teams went into extra innings in a 1–1 tie.

After a scoreless tenth, Travis Jackson led off the Giants' eleventh with a base hit and Gus Mancuso bunted him to second. Then Ryan, a light hitter, swung late at a fast ball and banged it to right field to send Jackson home and put the Giants ahead. Joe replaced the tired Weaver with Jack Russell, who slammed the door on the Giants, but it was too late. Hubbell held the Senators scoreless in the eleventh and the Giants won a 2–1 victory, putting them two games in front.

"We're still not licked," Joe insisted. "They've got to beat us four times to win this thing, and they've won only three. We'll get 'em tomorrow."

It was Crowder against Schumacher again, just as in the second game, but neither pitcher lasted beyond the sixth. Joe yanked Crowder after Schumacher drove in Mancuso in the Giants' sixth to give them a 3–0 lead, since they had already scored twice in the second inning. But the Senators got back into the ball game in their half of the sixth when, with two out, Cronin and Manush singled and Schulte smashed a three-run homer to tie it up. That finished Schumacher, who was replaced by Dolf Luque.

The relief pitchers were more effective than their predecessors, and by the end of the ninth the game was still tied at 3–3. For the second straight day, a World Series game went into extra innings.

The Giants settled it in the tenth with one swing of Mel Ott's bat. The little New York slugger, who hadn't had a hit all day, belted a home run into the right field seats that gave the Giants a 4–3 lead.

Joe still refused to give up. He came to bat with two out and nobody on in the last of the tenth and smashed a single through the box, and the Washington crowd perked up. When Luque walked Schulte, the fans really got excited, for now the Senators had the tying run on second and the winning run on first. But the Cuban relief pitcher fanned Kuhel, and it was all over.

Neither Joe nor his boys had anything to be ashamed of. One break in either of the last two games would have made all the difference in the world.

12.

For a dismal fifteen minutes or so, the loss of the series seemed the end of the world to Joe and his mates. Silent and disconsolate, they filed back to their locker room and sat in front of their lockers staring listlessly at their feet before beginning to peel off their uniforms. After consoling his men, Joe walked across the corridor to the jubilantly noisy Giants' locker room to congratulate Bill Terry.

Back with his own team, Joe was greeted by Clark Griffith.

"Sorry we let you down, Griff," he said.

"You didn't let anybody down," the owner replied. "Why, you fellows were great. Sure, it was tough to lose, but we'll be back in there again before long, and the next time the result will be different. You all did your best. Nobody can ask for more than that."

Then, putting an arm around Cronin, the old man added, "Just remember, Joe, win or lose, I'm with you."

"Thanks, Griff," Joe murmured, swallowing hard. "Thanks a lot."

He planned to leave for home two days later, but once

97

again Griffith called him into the office at the last minute.

"Before you go, Joe," his boss said, "how about signing this?"

It was a three-year contract, calling for twenty-three thousand dollars a year.

"Are you serious, Griff?" Joe asked. "Do you know what this means? We could finish in the cellar for the next two years and you'd still be stuck with me."

"I'll take my chances on that," Griffith said with a smile.

Joe signed, and Griffith immediately called in the baseball writers. "Gentlemen," he said, "I'm more than satisfied with Joe Cronin's work this year, and I'm proud to have this boy running my ball club."

With twenty-three thousand dollars a year for three years, Joe felt at last that he could ask Mildred to marry him. There were just a few personal matters to settle in San Francisco, and he would pop the question in the spring at Biloxi.

He traveled alone as far as Chicago, where he changed trains. From there to San Francisco he was with Lefty O'Doul, a veteran ballplayer who had starred as a pinch hitter for the Giants in the early games of the World Series. O'Doul was also from San Francisco. The two were to be given a reception on their arrival home.

They were met by a civic committee headed by Mayor Angelo J. Rossi, and for a while Cronin thought he had won the Series, not lost it. There was a parade, a presentation of keys to the city and a huge banquet, with Joe's relatives and O'Doul's as invited guests.

When it was all over, Joe told friends, "What a wonderful way to come home! No matter where I go, I can't imagine ever living anywhere else but in San Francisco."

He attended so many dinners that winter that his weight ballooned sky high. Although he began taking off some of the blubber before leaving for Biloxi, he still was fifteen pounds overweight when spring training began. Angry at himself for being so careless, Joe worked harder than ever that spring, but baseball wasn't the only thing on his mind.

Now that his parents were secure for the rest of their lives, it was time to ask Mildred to marry him. His proposal was hardly a surprise to her, any more than her acceptance was to him. They decided to be married as soon as the 1934 baseball season was over. Mildred, a Protestant, began taking instruction in the Catholic faith at once, in accordance with Joe's wishes.

Only their families and close friends were told of the engagement, which was never formally announced. Clark Griffith, of course, was delighted, and so was everyone else in his large family.

"I've always thought of you as my own son," he told Joe. "Now I'm glad you're practically becoming just that. There's no one in the world I'd rather see Mildred marry."

The Senators were almost unanimous choices to repeat their 1933 triumph, and Joe was as confident as anyone. The team looked good in spring training, everyone seemed healthy and the boys all had a year of championship experience behind them.

Then, out of a clear sky, Lady Luck, who had turned her best smile on Joe the year before, suddenly turned her back on him.

The first indication of trouble came when Luke Sewell, the Senators' first-string catcher, crushed his right index finger just before the club broke camp. Moe Berg replaced him behind the bat, and Cronin had to call Ed Phillips up from the minors in case of an emergency.

The Senators opened the season with Berg behind the plate and Johnny Stone, a good-hitting right fielder who had come to Washington from Detroit in a trade for Goslin. The rest of the Senators' opening day line-up was the same as it had been the year before, with Kuhel, Myer, Cronin and Bluege in the infield, and Schulte and Manush the other outfielders.

But neither Myer nor Cronin was up to par. Joe hurt his toe on the day before the opener, and Myer had had back trouble all through spring training. Earl Whitehill had been sick, but he pitched the first game of the year, although he needed help before it was over.

In spite of their troubles, the Senators beat the Red Sox in Boston, and Joe had hopes that things would improve. The team did fairly well for a week, then illness and injury began hitting again, and the Washington club became the Jonah of baseball.

Walter Stewart was out for nearly a month with abscessed teeth. Whitehill never felt completely himself. Joe suffered a sinus attack in May, but played anyhow. Myer's back was just beginning to come around when he got spiked in the foot and was out for two weeks. Heinie Manush suffered a recurrence of an old groin injury which put him on the shelf for two weeks, causing him to walk with a limp the rest of the season. Luke Sewell returned to the line-up just in time to get hit in the head with a pitched ball, knocking him out of action for another three weeks. Then Berg broke his little finger and Phillips, the green rookie, had to do the catching.

The clincher came in July when Joe Kuhel, the heavy-hitting first baseman, broke his leg. That put him out for the season, and the Senators' last hopes for a repeat of their 1933 pennant went out with him. By midseason, the Senators were in fifth place, and Joe had his doubts that they could finish in the first division.

He had some respite from his woes at All-Star time, for, as manager of the American League champions the year before, he automatically became manager of the American League team. He had the satisfaction of guiding the club to a 9–7 victory at the Polo Grounds in New York, where he got a single and a double and was the fielding star of the game. Joe handled ten chances perfectly, drove in a run and generally fired up the ball club.

He was also one of the victims in the most amazing pitching performance in All-Star game history. Carl Hubbell of the Giants fanned Babe Ruth, Lou Gehrig and Jimmy Foxx in the first inning, then opened the second by striking out Al Simmons and Joe Cronin. His five successive strikeouts of the greatest hitters in baseball still stands as an All-Star game record.

After the game, Joe returned to the business of trying to pull the harassed Senators together before it was too late. But the bad luck which had dogged them at the start of the season refused to go away. Joe benched Bluege, who wasn't hitting, for Cecil Travis, who began tearing opposing pitchers apart—until he got beaned and was lost for ten days. A week after his return, he strained a couple of ligaments and went back on the sick list for two more weeks.

The dismal streak never ended. Johnny Stone tore some ankle ligaments and was lost to the team for six weeks. Jack Russell was spiked in the foot. Dave Harris, a fine pinch hitter who could have played a lot of outfield that year, had an early-season Charley horse that never quite healed. Red Kress, a utility infielder, broke his thumb in August. Ed Linke, a promising young pitcher, came up with a sore arm.

"If it weren't so tragic," Joe told the writers one day, "it would be funny."

But there wasn't anything very funny about floundering around in sixth place and threatening to sink to seventh, which appeared to be the Senators' fate by early September.

By then, Joe was making do with what he had, living from day to day, using whoever was healthy.

The crowning blow came on Labor Day, when the Senators were playing a doubleheader against the Red Sox in Washington. In the eighth inning of the first game, Joe hit a dribbler down the first base line. As he charged toward the bag, Wes Ferrell, the Red Sox pitcher, came over to field the ball. The two crashed and Joe went down, turned several somersaults and landed on his right arm.

It bothered him somewhat, but he finished the game, even handling a relay throw from the outfield in the ninth inning. In the clubhouse afterward, it hurt so badly that he went to the hospital for X rays. Only then did he find out that he had played half an inning with a broken wrist. That was the end of the season as far as Joe was concerned.

Al Schacht took the team west, but Joe joined the club as soon as he was out of the hospital. It was a dismal trip. The Senators, with Schulte and Bluege the only regulars to stay healthy all year, were a patchwork ball club. They dropped to seventh place and never came out.

On their return to Washington, Griffith said, "Joe, we've just got to write this season off. You're through for the year and so is the ball club. If you'd like to take the last week off and get married that much sooner, it's perfectly all right with me."

"I'm not a quitter, Griff," Joe muttered.

"This isn't quitting," Griffith declared. "This is just common sense. There's no purpose in your going through the motions. We can't move up and we can't move down, so Al can get the club through the rest of the season. Besides—" Griffith grinned "—well—I was talking it over with Mildred while you fellows were away—"

Joe looked at the old man and grinned back. "You don't happen to know what date she picked, do you?" he asked.

"September 27," Griffith replied.

With the members of the ball club as guests, Joe and Mildred were married at St. Matthew's Church in Washington on September 27. The wedding got Joe off the sports pages and into the society columns of the newspapers for several days. It also made him a hero all over again, for the idea of the boy manager marrying the boss's daughter couldn't help but capture the imagination.

A huge crowd of fans and well-wishers was on hand as the couple came out of the church, and there were more people at the railroad station when they left for New York. There, they took a leisurely cruise to San Francisco, a trip that would keep them practically incommunicado for nearly a month.

When Mildred and Joe Cronin embarked on their honeymoon, he was the manager of the Washington Senators, with two more years to go on his contract. Not until he arrived in San Francisco did he have the slightest inkling that a radical change in his status was waiting only for his approval to be consummated.

13.

With his bride beside him on the deck of their honeymoon ship, Joe caught his breath with pride as the lovely Golden Gate, partly obscured by an early morning fog, first hove into view. San Francisco never looked more beautiful to him, and words of admiration came tumbling from his lips as he described in detail the sights that unfolded before them. There were the hills of Marin County to the left, the seal rocks of Land's End on the right, the great copper-colored Golden Gate Bridge dead ahead and, beyond that, like a huge ship in the middle of the bay, the prison island of Alcatraz.

The ship docked and the young couple was greeted by Joe's family and a few close friends. Not until hours later did Mildred have time to call her own family in Washington. Only then did Joe learn that Clark Griffith had been trying for days to reach him. He called the Senators' owner at the ball park as soon as Mildred hung up.

The old man, his voice quivering with emotion, went right to the point. "Joe," he said quietly, "Tom Yawkey has offered me Lyn Lary and a quarter of a million dollars for you."

Joe laughed. "Griff," he kidded, "come back to earth. Nobody offers that much for anyone."

"It's true, Joe. He wants you to manage the Red Sox. He's made up his mind to get you at any cost."

"But a quarter of a million dollars!" Joe's own voice was now vibrant with wonder.

"I'm going to accept, Joe. I've got to."

"But I don't want to leave you, Griff."

"I hate to see you go, Joe," the other agreed, "but this is a once-in-a-lifetime chance for both of us. It's nearly twice as much money as the Yankees paid for Babe Ruth, and probably more than anyone will ever again pay for a single ballplayer. I'd be crazy to turn it down, and so would you. Yawkey will pay you far more than I did, and he can do more for you in the future than I could. Besides, he'll give you a five-year contract."

Joe whistled. "Unbelievable," he whispered. "Absolutely unbelievable!"

"Well, Yawkey wants a winner and he's willing to go that high for one," said Griffith. "I think we'd better make the deal."

"Okay, Griff. Whatever you want to do is all right with me."

After telling Mildred and the family about this sudden change in his fortunes, the first thing Joe did was call Boston. He couldn't reach Yawkey, but he talked at length to Eddie Collins, the Red Sox general manager. Yawkey phoned him later in the day, and they all agreed to meet at the winter meetings.

In San Francisco, a reporter asked Mildred how she'd like living in Boston instead of Washington during the baseball season. "I'll be happy wherever Joe is," she answered. "I don't care if it's Boston, Washington, San Francisco or Oshkosh."

She and Joe rented a house on Monterey Boulevard, not far from the home Joe had bought for his parents in the Balboa Terrace section of San Francisco. Mildred, a refreshing young lady with a smile as broad as Joe's, made friends quickly, and within a few weeks felt as if she had lived in San Francisco all her life.

In the meantime, her husband acquainted himself with the problems of Tom Yawkey's Red Sox, who had so suddenly become his own responsibility.

The 1934 team had finished fourth under Bucky Harris, and it needed plenty of help if it were to go much higher. Yawkey had paid the Athletics one hundred thousand dollars the year before for Lefty Grove, but unfortunately the great southpaw immediately came up with a sore arm, winning only eight games. Wes Ferrell, volatile and hot tempered, won fourteen, a rookie named Johnny Welch thirteen, Dusty Rhodes twelve and the rest of the hurlers straggled along behind. Obviously, the ball club would win no pennants with that kind of a pitching staff.

The infield wasn't in the best of shape either. The Red Sox had been trying to get Jimmy Foxx from Philadelphia, but manager Connie Mack wasn't in a hurry to part with the slugging first baseman. Foxx, a right-handed hitter who had once belted fifty-eight home runs, was made for Boston's Fenway Park, which had a short left field wall built for right-handed power.

Joe knew the wall would help him, just as he knew his own fielding would make a big difference in an infield that had been shaky. The Red Sox had started the 1934 season with Max Bishop at second, Billy Werber at short and Bucky Walters, who later became a great pitcher for the Phillies and the Reds, at third. Eventually Werber was shifted to third base, and he would play there for Joe in 1935. Bishop would remain at second, Joe at short and the first baseman would be a rookie named Babe Dahlgren, whom the Red Sox purchased during the winter meetings right after Joe joined the club.

Rick Ferrell, Wes's brother, was one of the best catchers in the American League, and a pretty fair outfield was available to Joe from among Roy Johnson, Dusty Cooke, Carl Reynolds, Bing Miller, Mel Almada and Julius Solters. Yet because of the pitching staff, this was still no better than a fourth-place ball club.

Having played against most of the players, Joe was acquainted with everyone but the rookies. He didn't anticipate any serious problems, but he wasn't sure he could whip this team into the kind of inspired champions his 1933 Senators had been. There were too many veterans, jaded by a long succession of so-so years and now spoiled by a too-generous owner.

Tom Yawkey was convinced of two things—ballplayers could do no wrong and practically all of them should get raises every year. The Red Sox magnate, only a year or two older than Cronin, was baseball's leading hero-worshiper. No one, not even Eddie Collins, a once-great star whom Yawkey adored, could get him to understand that ballplayers weren't perfect and might take advantage of his good nature.

With Griffith's permission, Joe took Al Schacht to Boston with him as a coach. He also purchased Moe Berg from the Senators as a second-string and bull pen catcher. Berg was an amazing character who spoke fourteen languages, held a law degree and had taken a Master's degree at the Sorbonne in Paris after his graduation with honors from Princeton. One of the few ballplayers who made more money off the field than on it, Berg was in baseball only because he loved the game. He was a good catcher who missed being an outstanding star only because he couldn't hit.

Joe met his new ball club at Sarasota, Florida, for spring training. His hopes were high for the future, but he couldn't expect much to happen in 1935. There just wasn't enough talent available. Furthermore, this was not so much a team as a collection of unusual individuals, not all of whom had their minds on baseball alone. Some liked to go out on the town, others were "clubhouse lawyers," still others were temperamental.

The two top pitchers, Wes Ferrell and Lefty Grove, were in this last category. Ferrell had a dreadful temper. Grove was a moody man who loved Yawkey and respected Collins and Cronin but went into long fits of depression. Billy Werber, bright, strong-minded and a practical joker, was another man who did pretty much as he pleased.

Except for a wrist sprain which he suffered in an exhibition game against the Tigers at Lakeland, Joe had no troubles in Florida. By the time he took the team north, the injury wasn't serious enough to keep him out of action.

The Red Sox got off to a fantastic start. Ferrell threw a two-hitter on opening day, edging the Yankees and Lefty Gomez, 1–0, in a thriller at Yankee Stadium. They made it two straight in another thriller that went ten innings the next day. Then they headed for Washington, and Joe's debut as a visiting manager there.

Washington! Scene of his greatest triumphs, his happiest moments, his second home for seven years. This had been *his* town, *his* team—and now he was returning as an enemy baseball alien.

Al Schacht sat beside him on the train as it approached the city. As if reading Joe's thoughts, he asked, "How does it feel?"

"Funny—funny as can be. But do you know what, Al?

Much as I love the old man, I want to beat his team's brains out."

"Sure you do," the other nodded. "And so do I. When you get that uniform on, you want to strangle your own brother—unless he's wearing the same uniform."

Schacht was right. The moment Joe donned the visiting gray uniform of the Boston Red Sox, he forgot where he was. The only thing that counted was to win. Once on the field, Joe thought of nothing else.

Just to prove it, he personally led the Red Sox to their third straight triumph, raking Washington pitching for a double and a triple. Then, after splitting the next two games, he and his hot ball club traveled to Boston with a record of four victories and one defeat in their first five games. With home crowds cheering them on, Cronin and his boys belted the Yankees twice in a row again, giving them the undisputed leadership of the league.

By the end of the first week of the season, Boston fans were already talking pennant, but they were whistling in the dark, for the Red Sox were nowhere near that good. The ball club began settling back to its normal pace, and soon the Yankees and Tigers were both ahead of them.

In the meantime, Joe had his own troubles. He made three errors behind Lefty Grove one day, while the fans booed and Grove sulked. Cronin was worried about his pitching, which, after Grove and Ferrell, was unbelievably bad. Max Bishop had slowed up so much that Joe knew he had to get another second baseman as soon as possible. The club had some power, but not enough.

In mid-May, the Red Sox traded Solters to the St. Louis Browns for Oscar Melillo, and that eased the second base problem for the time being. But although the team showed occasional flashes of brilliance, it wasn't getting anywhere and Joe was quite aware that in its present form it never would.

Yet 1935 was an interesting season, which produced thrills for Cronin both on and off the field. Nearly 1000 people flocked to a testimonial banquet for him at the Copley Plaza Hotel in late May. Boston's loyal Red Sox fans might boo Joe when he made playing errors, but they took the smiling Irishman and his charming wife right to their hearts. City and state dignitaries were among those present at the banquet and Joe was overwhelmed with gratitude and delight.

For the first time in his life, he contemplated living permanently out of San Francisco.

"Someday," he told Mildred, "I think we might move here. The town is great and so are the people. I'd really feel at home here."

"So would I," Mildred agreed.

After helping the American League All-Stars win their third straight victory from the National League in Cleveland, where the game was played that year, Joe returned to Boston to try to move the Red Sox up in the standings. The outlook wasn't hopeful. The Red Sox were in fourth place and destined to stay there. The individualists continued to think of themselves first, with the team coming second. Werber, a marvelous base stealer, drove Joe crazy with the chances he took. More than one rally was killed when the fast third baseman got picked off trying to take an extra base. Yet Joe didn't object too strenuously, for he liked Werber's spirit and knew it was good for the ball club to have a man like that around.

In early August Cronin gave Boston fans one of the thrills of the year. The Red Sox were trailing the Yankees, 5–3, when he came to bat against pitcher Johnny Broaca with two men out and two on in the ninth. The first pitch was right across the letters and Joe smashed it over the left field fence to break up the ball game. The place was a bedlam as he crossed the plate with the winning run.

He had another great afternoon during the Labor Day doubleheader against the Senators at Fenway Park. The Red Sox won the first game in eleven innings, 9–6, as Joe, with a single, a double and a grand slam home run, batted in six runs. He had two doubles and a single in the second game, which went thirteen innings before the Senators finally won it.

One afternoon in September, in a game against the Indians in Boston, Joe was involved in a play that is seldom seen in baseball. The Red Sox were losing, 5–3, when they got the bases full with nobody out in the ninth inning. When Joe came to bat, Almada was on first, Werber on second and Dusty Cooke on third.

Joe hit a vicious line drive inside the third base line which seemed ticketed for two bases, and everybody started running. Sammy Hale, the Cleveland third baseman, barely had time to get his glove up in front of his face, and the ball skittered off it. Billy Knickerbocker, the shortstop, grabbed it before it hit the ground, and Cronin was out. Knickerbocker then threw to Roy Hughes, the second baseman, who touched second to retire Werber, then relayed the ball to Hal Trosky at first, getting Almada before he could slide back to the bag.

Thus, by a lucky break, the Indians transformed the hit that might have won the ball game into a triple play. It served as a fit climax to a campaign which had had its daffy moments. Two weeks later the season was all over with the Red Sox finishing fourth, just where they had been the year before, and Joe an older, wiser man.

Something had to be done to bolster the pitching staff. It was true that Grove, substituting control and wile for the speed that he had lost, won twenty games, and that Wes Ferrell, with all his temper tantrums, had an amazing year, winning twenty-five games. But no other hurler was outstanding. Johnny Welch won ten games and the others had nondescript records. Furthermore, Grove and Ferrell were getting no younger, and Grove's arm was always a question mark.

Before going home to San Francisco, Joe was in conference with Eddie Collins a number of times, and the two were in constant touch with Yawkey by telephone. They all agreed that the team needed pitching and more right-handed power to take advantage of the left field fence. Yawkey gave them permission to spend as much as necessary in order to build up the team.

When Joe left Boston, he and his bosses had one big objective in mind—to get Jimmy Foxx from Philadelphia, regardless of price. There were signs that Connie Mack, the venerable owner of the Athletics, was getting ready to let the slugging first baseman go, and the Red Sox had no intention of letting anyone else outbid them.

They made the deal in December, sending two players and one hundred and fifty thousand dollars to the A's for Foxx and Johnny Marcum, a right-handed pitcher. The next day they traded Carl Reynolds and Roy Johnson to Washington for Joe's old roommate Heinie Manush. A month after that, they sent a couple of young pitchers and another bundle of cash to Philadelphia for second baseman Eric McNair and outfielder Doc Cramer.

When he met his team in Sarasota for spring training in 1936, Joe was confident that he had a potential winner—if the pitching held up!

112

14.

JOE WENT TO SPRING TRAINING IN 1936 WITH HIGH HOPES FOR the season to come. In the great Jimmy Foxx he had the long-hitting right-handed first baseman he felt was essential to a club playing half its games in Fenway Park. In Eric McNair he had an experienced young second baseman who figured to be around for several years. In Heinie Manush and Doc Cramer he had a couple of outfielders who weren't just hitters, but knew how to catch the ball, too. And in Johnny Marcum he had a pitcher who had won seventeen games for the last-place Athletics in 1935.

"If I can only whip these guys into a unit," he told Collins in Sarasota, "we might do some business."

"Get tough with them, Joe," Collins said. "That's the only way to handle them."

So Joe got tough. He dressed down the clubhouse lawyers and the bad actors, fining them when he had to. Eventually, he had them pretty well under control, but there was another problem not quite so easy to solve. He found it hard to discipline the comedians and the musicians and the practical jokers, because they really weren't doing anything wrong—were just having fun. And in spite of himself, Joe often found himself laughing and having fun with them, for they were only doing what he would have liked to do himself if he were not the boss.

Doc Cramer was an incomparable mimic, particularly clever at imitating voices. Sometimes he would call another ballplayer and keep him on the phone for an hour or more. And whenever Joe tried to be angry, the curly-haired outfielder broke him up with a fast imitation of somebody else on the ball club.

Cramer, Cooke and Werber were fun-loving types who greeted people with electric buzzers in their hands, knotted bed sheets in train berths, put tacks on chairs, gave an unsuspecting player a hotfoot, spread itching powder around, and indulged in whatever other type of horseplay that came into their heads. They laughed at themselves and everyone else, and all too often their harassed young manager laughed with them.

The Ferrells were talented musicians. They owned mandolins, banjos, guitars and ukeleles and could play all of them interchangeably. Oscar Melillo was fascinated by them and finally let them talk him into buying an accordion, even though he had never played one. With the help of the brothers, he learned so fast that Joe commented one day, "If some of these guys would put as much effort into winning as they do into other things, maybe we'd get somewhere."

Yet the Ferrells and Melillo helped their teammates while away countless hours in trains, and Joe couldn't be too hard on them. Outside of forbidding them from turning the locker room into a concert hall, he made no serious attempt to stop them. Anyhow he enjoyed listening to them himself.

Another problem Joe had to contend with were the few

114

ballplayers who completely ignored the fundamentals of training routine. When Joe caught them meandering into hotel lobbies at all hours of the night, he cracked down on them. He seldom caught them, however, because he had to keep in trim himself, and also hated the thought of making spies out of his coaches.

There was one other problem which Joe never mentioned either then or later, but it was obvious to close observers of the ball club. Tom Yawkey was so fond of his players that he was willing to let them get away with almost anything. More than once, he quietly returned or rescinded fines imposed by Cronin. Through no fault of his own, Joe soon acquired a reputation of being too softhearted to discipline his ballplayers. Actually, Joe *was* softhearted, but he could be tough and often was. Collins always backed him up, but Yawkey didn't want to see anyone's feelings hurt.

With such a motley collection of personalities, Joe needed more than his share of luck to keep them out of the second division, but in 1936 he had very little. His troubles began on the day the Red Sox arrived in Boston for the opening of the season. That morning Johnny Marcum woke up with terrible stomach pains and before the day was over, his appendix had to be removed.

The Red Sox opened at home against the Athletics. Halfway through the second game of the series, Joe broke his thumb tagging out Philadelphia's Mike Higgins. That should have put him on the shelf for several weeks, but he refused to stay out of action. Less than a week after the mishap he was back at shortstop, wearing a rubber splint on the ailing finger.

As the season progressed, all his hopes went down the drain. Even after recovering from his operation, Marcum never regained his 1935 form, and won only eight games. Ferrell won twenty but lost fifteen, and the slipping Grove won seventeen and lost twelve. The lone bright spot in the pitching was provided by Fritz Ostermueller, who won sixteen games.

Jimmy Foxx batted .338 and hit forty-one home runs, but it was a poor season for him. More than once he went to Joe and said, "Gee, Mr. Yawkey spent all that money for me and look what he got. I don't know what's wrong with me."

"Don't you worry, Jimmy," Joe reassured the veteran, "you're doing fine. I wish the others did as well."

The club sank into the second division and stayed there. Joe tried to find some answers during his frequent conferences with Eddie Collins and Tom Yawkey as they went over and over the Red Sox roster.

"We've *got* to have pitching," Joe said. "Ferrell can't do everything and I don't know how much more we can expect from Grove."

"The farm system is coming along," Collins said. "It will start paying off in a few years. In the meantime, I'll buy ballplayers wherever I can find them."

"Don't worry about what positions they play," Joe commented. "We can always fit a good ballplayer in somewhere."

In July Collins went to San Diego on a scouting trip. "I'm particularly interested in George Myatt," he told Joe. "If he's as good as they say, we'll buy him and worry about where to play him later."

Myatt was a shortstop who had hit well in the Pacific Coast League. A dozen clubs were after him, and Collins, with carte blanche from Yawkey to spend as much as he had to, was ready to buy him. But the Red Sox general manager was more cautious with Yawkey's money than Yawkey was himself. He refused to take Myatt sight unseen; he wanted to look at the youth himself.

116

A week later he told Joe over the phone, "They want an awful lot of money for this boy and I don't think he's worth it, so I'm going to pass him up. I got Gene Desautels for next year—he'll help our catching. And I saw a couple of kids who look so promising that I bought one and took an option on the other. The fellow I took is an eighteen-year-old second baseman named Bobby Doerr. The other boy is only seventeen, but he's got the most beautiful batting swing I ever saw. When he reaches his full growth he should be great."

"What's his name?" Joe asked.

"Ted Williams," Collins said.

Joe was pleased at the news that he would have some help for the future. But now he was beset by personal troubles. His mother was so desperately ill that he finally decided to go to San Francisco. She died in July, leaving a vacuum in his life that he knew would never be filled.

Sadly he returned to Boston to try to collect the remnants of his shattered hopes, but he had difficulty picking up his own spirits, much less anyone else's. The season ended at last, with the Red Sox still anchored in sixth place.

Back in San Francisco that autumn, Joe refused to stay down. "Next year," he told Mildred. "There's always next year. Just a few breaks—a few pitchers—and we'll be all right."

He was his old cheerful self by the time he went east for the winter meetings, and he had a new reason for looking forward to the spring. Mildred was expecting a baby, and Joe was already dreaming about a new generation of Cronins in the major leagues.

When he met Collins and Yawkey in December, all three agreed that it was foolish to try any longer to buy a pennant. The Red Sox had the potential to win eventually, because

117

there were promising youngsters in the farm system who would be ready in a few years. Joe and his bosses went to the winter meetings with the purse strings pulled tight and waited to see what would happen.

Actually they swung only one deal, sending Werber to the Athletics for Mike Higgins. It was a straight player swap, with no money involved. Higgins was a strong right-handed hitter and a good fielder, although not as flashy as Werber. This didn't bother Joe, for he had already spent two years too many watching Werber take rash chances on the bases.

Just before going to Sarasota for the 1937 season, Joe got word that Eric McNair's wife had died in childbirth. Joe wired condolences, then started worrying about Mildred. She laughed at his fears, but that didn't make him feel any easier.

"I won't be completely happy until it's all over," he told her.

A month later, Mildred, who was expecting twins, lost them both when they arrived prematurely in a Sarasota hospital. For twenty-four hours, her own life was in danger, but she finally recovered.

Because of McNair, Joe hid his own grief. Somehow he managed to get through the saddest spring training season of his life.

In the meantime, the ball club really looked far better than it had the year before. While Higgins was not spectacular, he was a solid, steady third baseman. Desautels backed up Rick Ferrell so well that the Red Sox toyed with the idea of using the veteran receiver in a trade if an advantageous one could be arranged. And Doerr, even though only nineteen, was so impressive that Joe decided to keep him with the team, instead of farming him out.

"He'll learn more up here than he can in the minors,"

Joe said. "And I can use him in spots. By next year he'll be ready for a regular job."

The season began with Foxx, McNair, Cronin and Higgins in the infield and Cooke, Cramer and Manush in the outfield, with Rick Ferrell behind the bat. The Red Sox got away to a fair start, but by May they were looking for help on the mound and in the outfield.

The trouble was that Wes Ferrell had apparently lost his ability to win in Fenway Park. The right-hander was so ineffective that he soon lost twice as many games as he won.

"Let's try to peddle the Ferrells together," Joe suggested.

Collins agreed. In June he sent the brothers and Mel Almada to Washington for Buck Newsom and Ben Chapman. Newsom, even though an eccentric character, was such a fine right-handed pitcher that Joe decided he could put up with foibles if the man won ball games. Chapman was not only a great outfielder and a good hitter, but a fiery ballplayer, the type Joe liked and knew was needed on the club. He never forgot the fight Chapman had had with Buddy Myer in Washington, and was pleased at the idea of having a man like that on his own team.

The season turned out to be a poor one, though not as bad as 1936. Jimmy Foxx, plagued by sinus headaches, staggered along on his nerve. He played one hundred and fifty games, but was in agony a good part of the time, ending up with a .285 batting average and only thirty-six home runs. But Higgins and Cramer hit over .300 and so did Joe, who batted .307. The pitching staff was somewhat improved and better balanced than it had been in the previous two years. Grove ended up with seventeen victories, duplicating his 1936 performance, and Jack Wilson won sixteen, while Marcum and Newsom checked in with thirteen apiece.

The Red Sox finished fifth, but prospects for 1938 were much better. If Foxx could shake off the effects of his sinus

119

condition and Doerr turned out to be as good as he looked, things might perk up.

Just before Joe left for home, Collins said, "I exercised the option on that boy, Ted Williams. He'll be at Sarasota next spring."

Joe looked forward to meeting the youth.

15.

JOE WAS DETERMINED TO GET RID OF BUCK NEWSOM, WHO WAS not a good influence on young ballplayers. There were enough unusual personalities on the ball club already. Newsom, who ignored training rules, only added to the confusion in the few months that he had been around. Furthermore, his won-lost record of 13–10 hardly made up for his off-the-field behavior. If Joe were to put up with eccentric characters, they would have to do better than that. Eddie Collins agreed with him thoroughly. As soon as the 1937 season was over, the Red Sox general manager began shopping around for someone who would take Newsom in return for a pitcher or an outfielder, preferably a quiet, dependable athlete.

During the December meetings, the St. Louis Browns were glad to have Newsom. In return for him and two other ballplayers, the Browns gave up Joe Vosmik, who, along with Cramer and Chapman, gave the Red Sox an outfield which would be as good as any in the American League. All three could hit and all were good defensively.

121

After spending part of the winter in San Francisco and the rest in Washington, Joe left Mildred with the Griffiths when he went south for spring training in 1938. His wife was expecting again—and this time they were taking no chances of losing the baby. She would not do any traveling until it arrived.

Joe had a right to be more optimistic than ever as spring practice began. He had two new right-handed batters in Vosmik and Bobby Doerr, who could hit the short left field fence at Fenway Park and occasionally drive a ball over it. Doerr had spent the entire 1937 season with the Red Sox, appearing in only fifty-five games. While his batting average was not high, he hit a couple of home runs, showing signs of power, and had the same drive and determination which had inspired Joe in his rookie days. Better still, Doerr had become a smooth second baseman, good enough to displace Eric McNair. Since the youngster was only twenty, he figured to be around for a few years.

Two days after Cronin's arrival at Sarasota, Doerr walked into Joe's office off the locker room at Payne Field, followed by a fuzzy-cheeked youth with a shy smile, curly brown hair and a lanky build. Doerr shook hands with his boss, then introduced his companion.

"This is Ted Williams," he said. "We just drove in from the Coast."

"Glad to know you, Ted," smiled Joe. The tall kid grinned back, and immediately Joe was drawn to him. The youngster had an electric personality and even at eighteen he seemed to fill the room with his magnetism.

"Go and get ready for work, fellows," Joe said. "There's a lot to be done."

The kid could not only play ball, but he charmed everyone he met. The newspapermen went wild about him, and he, in turn, gave them plenty to write about. Fresh, friendly, bright and articulate, he said what he pleased, and within a week he was the talk of the training camp. The lanky rookie got a kick out of everything—the manager, the other ballplayers, the writers, the fans, the food, the hotel, everything about spring training. And, Joe noticed with satisfaction, he could hit a ball a mile.

But there were rough spots. A few weeks after spring training began, Joe and Collins sat down with some of the scouts to go over the rookies on the roster. When they reached Williams's name, Joe commented, "He's certainly a fine prospect, but I don't think he's quite ready for the big leagues yet. He's only a year and a half out of high school, and he's had just one full season in the minors. After one more, he'll be great."

"I agree," Collins added. "This fellow hit twenty-three homers at San Diego last year, but he didn't bat .300 and he struck out a lot. He'll be a great ballplayer—I'm sure of that. But there's no sense rushing him, especially since we don't need him this year."

So it was decided to send Williams to the Minneapolis Millers, with whom the Red Sox had a working agreement. The Millers trained at Avon Park, Florida, and Donie Bush, their manager, was in Sarasota to pick out ballplayers whom the Red Sox wouldn't be able to use for his team.

Bush, who sat in on the meeting, practically drooled when the decision was made. "I'll drive the kid over to Avon Park myself," he declared. "I want to get him out of here before you guys change your minds."

The two left that day, and Cronin didn't see Williams for another year. In the meantime, Joe concentrated on the coming season of 1938, hoping that this would be the year the Red Sox would really become a threat for the pennant.

Aside from the improvement brought about by the addition of Vosmik and Doerr, there were other signs of hope.

Jimmy Foxx was in perfect shape, with no evidence of the sinus condition which had plagued him the previous year. The infield of Foxx, Doerr, and Higgins was potentially the best Joe had ever played with, and it was certainly the most dangerous at the plate. All four were right-handed hitters capable of taking full advantage of the short left field fence.

The pitching was as spotty as ever, but Joe hoped that the club's batting power might make up for it. One surprising development was the attitude of Lefty Grove. The grizzled veteran was much more amiable in spring training than he had ever been before, and Joe noticed that he actually kidded with his teammates, which he had never done in the past.

The change was due to Tom Yawkey's influence. Grove and the youthful Red Sox owner were close friends, who often went hunting together during the winter. Yawkey had spent hours telling Grove how much he might help younger players if he didn't scare them to death.

"Not only that," Yawkey always added, "you'll feel better yourself."

The change in Grove was another step in easing Joe's handling of the ball club. The team was now quite different from the collection of problem children he had first met in 1935. There were still a few characters around, but most of the troublemakers were gone. Steady men like Mike Higgins, Gene Desautels, Bobby Doerr, Jimmy Foxx and Joe Vosmik, hard workers and serious ballplayers, were giving the Red Sox a new outlook.

"If we don't do well this year," Joe wrote Mildred, "it won't be because of a poor attitude. These fellows really want to play—and to win."

Joe's primary target was the Yankees. Under manager Joe McCarthy and sparked by Joe DiMaggio, they had won

124

two world's championships in a row and were favored to win the 1938 pennant as well. Day after day, as the season got under way, Joe stood in front of his ballplayers in the locker room and exclaimed, "Beat the Yankees and we beat them all!"

In spite of ineffectual pitching, the Red Sox got off to a great start. They won ball games with scores of twelve to ten and fourteen to eleven, with Joe using a parade of pitchers, but they won. The bull pen was always busy.

Sometimes, however, someone would last through a game, giving the bull pen crew a rest. Black Jack Wilson and Fritz Ostermueller were both capable of finishing the games they started, and Grove, his arm gone but his head still working, was far from through. These were the men out of whom Joe got the most, but he was never sure of them. Each of them could pitch a great game one day yet get knocked out of box the next.

Still, the team had started well, and Joe was happier than at any time since coming to Boston. He worried about his pitchers, but he worried far more about Mildred, who was in Washington waiting for her baby. The child, a healthy boy, arrived on May 6. He was named Thomas Griffith Cronin, after the two men closest to Joe during his baseball career. Joe celebrated the next day by hitting a home run off Bob Feller of the Indians in a game at Boston.

Now he could concentrate on his ball club. The Red Sox were putting up a real battle, fighting the Yankees every inch of the way. The race was so close that baseball fans all over the country were talking about Cronin's team when it went to New York for a May 30 doubleheader. "If the Red Sox had steady pitching, they'd win the pennant," a wire service baseball reporter wrote just before the big Yankee Stadium doubleheader, and many experts around the nation agreed with him.

125

With the Red Sox threatening to knock the Yankees off the top of the league standings, the fans flocked to the ball park for the Memorial Day bargain bill. By the time the first game started, there were 83,533 people on hand, and, judging by the backing the Red Sox had, thousands of them were from Boston. Indeed, many had come to New York especially for the series.

Lefty Grove was the starting pitcher for the Red Sox in the first game. Before it began, Joe went from man to man in the dugout, spreading his own infectious spirit about.

"Don't let them get away with *anything*," he exhorted. "Fight 'em all the way!"

The fighting began almost at once. After the Yanks got a man on base in the first inning, Jake Powell came to bat. Powell was a rough base runner who always came in spikes first, and had already just missed cutting up Bobby Doerr a couple of times in previous games. Now, as he stood at the plate, Grove threw a fast ball right at him, and the Yankee batter went down in a heap.

He got up slowly and yelled at the veteran left-hander, but Grove paid no attention to him. Powell hit the next pitch for a single, and when the next man up also got a hit, Powell barreled into second with both feet high and Doerr had to step lively to move out of the way. The youngster said nothing, however, for this was the sort of thing he expected, but Joe made a few uncomplimentary remarks as Powell headed for the dugout.

By the time Powell came up again, Grove had been replaced on the Red Sox mound by Arch McKain and the Red Sox were far behind. McKain's first pitch knocked Powell down, and he came up muttering to himself. When the next pitch, low and tight, caromed off Powell's shins, Jake blew his stack.

Dropping his bat, he went after McKain, who stood on the

126

mound waiting for him. But before Powell got there, Joe rushed over, pushed McKain out of the way, dropped his glove and squared off. While the fans howled with excitement, Cronin and Powell fought all over the infield, throwing punches and ignoring the efforts of ballplayers and umpires alike to separate them.

Cooler heads finally prevailed, and both were thrown out of the ball game. Joe stopped to talk to Al Schacht about pitchers for the second game, then headed for the showers. Powell was waiting for him under the stands.

The two went at it again, this time in comparative privacy, and it was a full minute before they were noticed. Once again it took half a dozen men from both teams to separate them.

Later, one of the Red Sox players remarked, "I've seen fights before, but usually they're stopped before anybody lands a damaging punch. But that battle between Cronin and Powell was one of the best I ever saw, in or out of the ring."

Many weeks later the two shook hands, but witnesses to this intense battle never forgot it. Years later there were thousands of fans who remembered all the details of the fight, but couldn't say who won the ball games. As a matter of record, the Yankees won both, to stop the Red Sox' threatening drive.

If Joe had any detractors in Boston, they quieted down after his fight with Powell. Even though the Yankees went ahead to a prohibitive lead, few Red Sox fans booed Joe that year. And on September 7, a group of his loyal supporters put on a "day" for him at Fenway Park, giving him and Mildred a set of sterling silver, and Tommy a houseful of toys.

Before the game, Jimmy Foxx said over the loud-speaker system at the ball park, "I never enjoyed playing under any manager as much as under Joe." When it was Yawkey's turn to speak, he said, "Joe Cronin will be a part of the Red Sox organization as long as I'm connected with it."

Then, with Joe getting two hits, the Red Sox murdered the Yankees, 11–4.

But it was much too late to catch Joe McCarthy's club. When the season ended, the Yankees were nine and a half games in front. The Red Sox were second, and there was every hope of better things in the future for them.

Foxx had his greatest season in Boston and was voted the year's Most Valuable Player. He batted .349, collected fifty home runs and piled up a fantastic total of one hundred and seventy-five runs batted in, only nine short of Lou Gehrig's American League record.

While Foxx was the pace-setter, the entire Red Sox ball club clobbered the ball. Ben Chapman, temperamental but consistent, hit .340 and Joe himself had a .325 mark, his best in a Red Sox uniform. Every regular but Doerr and Desautels was over .300; Doerr, lowest on the list, batted .289. Thus the regulars had a team average of well over .300, so it took some very bad pitching indeed to keep them from winning the pennant.

Still, some of Joe's hurlers emerged with fairly good records. Grove won fourteen and lost four, but this was deceptive, for it didn't show the times he was knocked out of the box. The same was true of Ostermueller, who won thirteen and lost five. The real work horse of the staff was Jack Wilson, who won fifteen and lost fifteen. The rest of the pitchers straggled along behind, with the best mark of all by Joe Heving—eight wins and only one loss, all in relief. Inning for inning, he was the most effective pitcher on the ball club.

"It was a good season," Collins told Joe before the two

parted for the winter. "We made a lot of new fans, and maybe next year we can give them a winner."

"I sure hope so," Joe said. "It would help if a few other clubs knocked off the Yankees once in a while."

He had a point there. The Red Sox had held the Yankees even, with eleven victories and eleven defeats. All other teams in the league lost more games to the champions than they won.

16.

THERE WAS NO QUESTION ABOUT TED WILLIAMS BEING READY for the major leagues by the time the 1938 season was over. The youngster from San Diego hit .366 and belted forty-three home runs in Minneapolis, so the Red Sox could now spare an outfielder for trading purposes in their quest for pitching strength. They could spare Mike Higgins, too, because another hot youngster, Jim Tabor, who had played a few games at third base near the end of the season, was also ready.

The Red Sox went to market in December with ballplayers instead of money for bait, and made two deals for pitchers which they hoped would mean a 1939 pennant. They sent Higgins and Arch McKain to Detroit for three players, one of whom was Elden Auker, a fine right-handed submarine pitcher. Cleveland sent them Denny Galehouse and another player in exchange for Ben Chapman. Galehouse was a right-hander with only a fair record, but he could beat the Yankees.

Everyone in the Red Sox organization hated to see Higgins

130

go, for he had been an excellent team man as well as a good ballplayer. At the time the trade was made, Yawkey told Cronin and Collins, "Someday I want that fellow back. He's too good a man to lose permanently."

"Maybe someday we can use him again," Collins said, "but not right now."

"We can win the pennant with this ball club," Joe added.

It was indeed a potent team. Foxx, Doerr, Cronin and Tabor might well be the hardest-hitting quartet of right-handed infielders ever assembled. Cramer and Vosmik weren't sluggers, but they could get on base, and there seemed to be no limit to Williams' possibilities. Auker and Galehouse would bolster the sagging pitching staff, and Joe had hopes that Wilson and Ostermueller might yet develop into stars. He could count on Lefty Grove for occasional help only, and he had Joe Heving and Jim Bagby, Jr. for bull pen duty. The catching, which would be split between Gene Desautels and Johnny Peacock, was adequate, although not outstanding.

Once again Williams was the talk of the training camp. Brash and independent, the slender rookie was so colorful that writers from all over the country flocked to Sarasota just to see him. Fast with a quip and bubbling over with friendly enthusiasm, he continued to delight everyone he met, including the Boston baseball writers, who wrote reams of ecstatic copy about him.

He was so confident that Cronin had to caution him every once in a while. "There are some pretty good pitchers up here. Don't think it'll be so easy to hit them."

"I'll hit them, don't worry," Williams retorted. "I'm going to be the greatest hitter who ever lived."

"I'm with you," Joe laughed. "I hope you make 'em forget Ty Cobb and Babe Ruth and Joe DiMaggio and all the rest of them."

131

Sometimes he had to discipline the short-tempered young-ster. One day, while barnstorming north, a ball went by Williams during an exhibition game in Atlanta. Ted was so upset when he finally caught up with the ball that he picked it up and threw it over the fence. Joe was wild with rage. He ran out to right field and barked, "If you don't want to play, go back to the hotel." Hanging his head, Williams left the ball park.

A week later, in Baltimore, Joe had to speak to him again, this time for being too forceful as he yelled back at heckling fans. "You're in a big leagues now," Joe said icily. "Act like a big leaguer—and talk like one."

While he knew he would have to discipline the kid every so often, Cronin didn't want to do anything that would dis-courage him or rob him of his marvelous enthusiasm. "He's the greatest natural hitter I ever saw," Joe told Mildred after arriving in Boston. "And one of the freshest rookies I'll ever meet. But if he weren't so fresh he might not be such a great ballplayer. My problem is to try to keep him in line without holding him back."

Since this wasn't possible, Joe finally had to let Williams have his head. From then on, the Red Sox punished him only for his most flagrant breaches of etiquette.

The team got off to a fair start, but it wasn't good enough. The Yankees, led by the great DiMaggio, shot into an early lead, and were thirteen and a half games ahead of the Red Sox by early July. Then, for a brief and thrilling few days, it appeared as if Joe Cronin's boys might pull off the impossible. They began a winning streak the day after the Fourth of July, and had cut the Yankees lead to eleven and a half games when they came into New York for a five-game series—a single contest on Friday, July 7, and double-headers Saturday and Sunday.

Before the first game, Joe declared in the locker room,

"This is our chance. We'll be right back in the pennant race if we win this series. Let's knock these guys dead!"

He demonstrated by example. In the first inning, he drove Cramer home with a single for the first run of the game. With the Yankees ahead, 2–1, he led off the fourth with a home run into the left field stands off Red Ruffing to tie the score. On top of that, he was all over the infield. He never let up on his teammates, and they finally won, 4–3.

Joe inspired them again on Saturday. His long sacrifice fly drove Foxx home with the first run of the opening game, and the Red Sox took a 3–1 victory behind Ostermueller's fine pitching. In the second game, Joe broke a scoreless tie in the seventh inning by driving Foxx home again, this time with a single, and Galehouse pulled out a 3–2 triumph.

The Red Sox's three wins in a row inspired Boston fans to flock to New York for the Sunday doubleheader. The Yankees, frustrated and sore, had a 3–2 lead in the first game when Joe came to bat in the eighth inning with one out and Williams on first.

Monte Pearson, the big Yankee right-hander, threw a curve ball for a strike, and Joe stepped out of the batter's box. As he rubbed dirt on his hands, he remarked to Bill Dickey, the Yankees' catcher, "I should have murdered that, Bill. I wish he'd throw me another one." Then he hitched up his trousers, moved back in and looked for a fast ball.

The next pitch was high and outside for a ball. The count was one and one, and Joe watched Pearson narrowly as the pitcher leaned forward to get the sign from Dickey. The Yankee pitcher stretched, checked Williams' lead off first, then threw. It was a curve and, as it swerved toward the plate, Joe stepped into it. He swung a trifle late and the ball caromed foul.

Joe moved out of the box and bent down for more dirt.

As he straightened up, he commented to Dickey, "Boy, Monte's tough today. I was lucky to foul that one off."

In came another curve, missing the inside corner, and the count was two and two. Pearson stomped around the mound after Dickey tossed the ball back to him, then twice threw to first to keep Williams close to the bag. Joe fidgeted at the plate, hitching up his pants, wiggling his bat, touching his cap and flicking dirt with his spikes, first with one foot, then the other.

The pitch was high and outside and Joe let it go by for another ball. That made the count three and two, and there was a ripple of sighs from the stands. Dickey threw the ball to Pearson and Joe moved away from the box again. While the Yankee pitcher waited impatiently, he carefully rubbed his hands, stalling until the plate umpire ordered him back into the batter's box.

Once more Pearson stretched and checked first base. Before he drew his arm back to pitch, Joe thought, It'll be a fast ball. I can feel it in my bones.

Pearson finally poured it in. The instant it left his hand Joe knew this was the pitch he had been looking for—fast and right across the letters. Snapping his bat around, Joe met the pitch squarely and sent a screaming fly high and far in the direction of left center field. Neither George Selkirk, the Yankee left fielder nor Joe DiMaggio in center took more than a step or two. Then both stopped and watched the ball land in the visitors' bull pen. It was a home run all the way.

That was the ball game. The Red Sox won it, 4–3. Jimmy Foxx settled the second game with a home run into the left field stands and the Red Sox, who had come into town hopelessly far behind, left the Stadium only six and a half games in back of the shocked Yankees. They had swept a five-game series in the Yankees' own back yard, won seven of their last eight against the champions and apparently transformed a Yankee walkaway into a fairly close pennant race.

But that was their swan song. With the Yankees racking up every other team in the league and their own pitching no better than usual, the Red Sox never had a chance. The Yankees won the pennant by seventeen games and, for the second year in a row, Joe Cronin's ball club finished second.

It wasn't the fault of the hitters, for the Red Sox led the league in batting for the second straight year. The mighty Foxx batted .360 and had thirty-five homers. Williams enjoyed a fine rookie season, with thirty-one homers and a .327 average. Joe batted .308 and had nineteen homers, the most of his career. The four Red Sox infielders hit eighty circuit drives among them, and the team collected 124.

The pitching was still very bad. Auker couldn't win a game at Fenway Park and Galehouse, although he continued to beat the Yankees, could beat hardly any other club. Grove won fifteen games, but he had become a Sunday pitcher, needing long rests between starts.

Most frustrating of all was the inability of other teams in the league to whip the Yankees. The Red Sox, who won eleven out of nineteen games from the champions, were the only team to outplay them.

Ted Williams, despite his fine year, started feuding with the public near the close of the season. One afternoon he let a ground ball go between his legs. Thinking he was loafing, a few fans booed him, infuriating the youth. He yelled something back and was greeted by a chorus of hoots. When he ran down the steps of the dugout after the inning was over, he declared, "The heck with those people. I'll never tip my cap to them again."

He never did.

Just before the season ended, Tom Yawkey called Joe

into the office, handed him a piece of paper and said, "How about signing this, Joe."

It was a five-year contract with a large raise in pay. After thanking him, Joe remarked, "You know, Tom, it looks as if we're going to be here long enough to move here permanently."

"Why don't you?" Yawkey suggested.

Mildred thought it was an excellent idea, and they built a house on a lake in the Boston suburb of Newton. Both were thrilled, for it was the first home they had ever owned.

However, they visited San Francisco after the season was over, for Joe's father and brothers still lived there. One day Joe went over to Seals Stadium to watch an exhibition game. He wanted to look at a young outfielder who had been turned down by several other teams. The boy's name was Dom DiMaggio.

Youngest brother of Joe and Vince DiMaggio, this member of the clan seemed the least likely big league prospect of them all. He was small, wore glasses and looked more like a college professor than a ballplayer. But he had hit .360 in the Pacific Coast League in 1939, and Cronin refused to believe that anyone with that kind of a batting average in Triple A ball wasn't a major league prospect.

Joe sat in the stands long enough to see DiMaggio field a few balls and go to the plate a couple of times. He didn't get a hit, but Joe was thoroughly satisfied. Without any further delay, he went right to a phone booth and put in a call for Eddie Collins in Boston.

"Buy Dom DiMaggio," Joe said. "Glasses or no glasses, he's great."

"They want fifty thousand for him," Collins pointed out.

"A bargain at twice the price," Joe said.

The deal was made and Joe planned on an outfield of DiMaggio, Williams and Cramer. Vosmik, waived out of the league, was sold to Brooklyn and Auker, a failure in Boston, went to the St. Louis Browns. As the opening of the 1940 season approached, Joe, as always, had hopes that this might be the year.

It wasn't. To begin with, DiMaggio hurt his knee in spring training and couldn't open the season. He got back just in time to replace Ted Williams, injured in an outfield collision with Cramer. Foxx's old sinus trouble came back, but even though he could hardly see well enough to follow the flight of the ball, he played almost all season.

And Joe himself was slowing up. He was thirty-three years old and seven seasons of double duty as manager and shortstop were beginning to take their toll. He kept in shape and was as enthusiastic as ever, but he simply couldn't get around as fast as in former years.

"We're going to need a shortstop in another year or so," he told Collins. "I'm doing more harm than good."

"If we find one who does half the job you do, I'll be satisfied," Collins replied.

In spite of their troubles, the Red Sox got off to a good start. Jim Bagby beat the Yankees on opening day, and, with Joe fighting every inch of the way and trying to instill the same spirit into the others, they remained in the pennant race for two months. They still had a chance at the All-Star break in midseason, and Joe figured that if the pitching stood up they might make it.

But the pitching collapsed in the second half of the season. Grove, trying hard to land in the charmed victory circle of three hundred, could pitch only about once in ten days, and even then he wasn't effective. He won seven and lost six and was still seven games short of his goal when the season ended. Nobody won more than twelve games and only three hurlers won ten or more.

The Red Sox were practically out of the race by Labor

Day. It was an unfortunate year for them to fall apart because the Yankees, for the first time in five years, were no longer invincible. Detroit won the pennant after a close race with Cleveland while the Yankees dropped to third, their poorest finish in the nine years Joe McCarthy managed them.

On the last day of the season, the Red Sox dropped into a tie with the Chicago White Sox for fourth position. Ironically, Boston was only eight games behind the pennant-winning Tigers. The year before, the Red Sox had trailed the Yankees by more than twice as many, yet finished second.

"At least," penned a Boston writer, "they aren't bridesmaids any more. They didn't finish second."

17.

THE FOURTH-PLACE TIE FINISH OF 1940 DIDN'T WORRY THE RED Sox brain trust half as much as the passage of time. Grove was hanging on only in hopes of winning the seven games he needed for a career total of 300. The team was still badly in need of a couple of reliable pitchers, and the catching was weak. With Foxx on his way out, the quest for a heavy-hitting right-handed first baseman would begin all over again. And Joe was eager to find someone who could fill in at shortstop, at least, if not play there regularly.

Winter deals solved some of the problems. The Red Sox traded Cramer to Washington for outfielder Gee Walker, then turned Walker, Bagby and Desautels over to Cleveland for Frank Pytlak, Joe Dobson and Sammy Hale. Pytlak was a better catcher than Desautels, Dobson a solid right-handed pitcher and Hale a good utility infielder.

Before the winter meetings were over, the Red Sox bought Pete Fox, an experienced outfielder, from Detroit and Skeeter Newsome, a good-fielding but weak-hitting short-stop, from Baltimore in the International League. Joe also had high hopes that a big price paid by the Red Sox to San Diego for pitcher Dick Newsome, who had won twenty-three games in the Pacific Coast League in 1940, would pay off. Dick, no relation to Skeeter, was a rangy right-hander who could throw hard and get the ball over the plate.

Joe went south with the usual hopes that always sprang eternally in his heart during spring training. When he got there and found Foxx in better shape than he expected, then discovered that he himself wasn't as creaky as he thought, he really began to have confidence that perhaps 1941 *would* be the year he was waiting for.

He started the season with the same heavy-hitting infield that had been so potent in 1939—Foxx at first, Doerr at second, himself at short and Tabor at third. Williams, Di-Maggio and Fox were in the outfield and Pytlak was top catcher. Joe's pitching hopes rested on Dobson, Grove, Dick Newsome and two promising kids from the farm system—Charley Wagner, who had finished the 1940 season with the Red Sox, and Tex Hughson, a tall, fast right-hander.

The Red Sox started well, and as in 1940 they were in the pennant race for the first few months of the season. As the weeks went by, it was apparent that the Yankees would win easily, and interest in the Red Sox centered on the fortunes of two individuals, ancient Lefty Grove and youthful Ted Williams. The old southpaw looked pathetic as he reached for the magic three-hundred mark; the young slugger was threatening to become the last of a vanishing breed of .400 hitters.

While he wished the team would do better, Joe was rooting hard for them both. Grove started a game about every ten days, but rarely lasted more than a few innings. He managed to stagger far enough to get credit for half a dozen victories in the first two and a half months of the season, which enabled him to chalk up his two hundred and ninety-ninth game. After that, the three-hundredth game seemed more elusive than ever.

Week after week, the forty-one-year-old southpaw got shelled by the opposition and finally had to leave before he had pitched the required five innings. His earned-run average soared to over 4.00 as he continued to reach for what began to appear unattainable. Several times he seemed on the verge of making it, but his ancient arm had lost its magic.

Three or four times Grove went to Joe and said, "Look, I'm not helping the ball club any. It's costing games when I start. Never mind the three-hundredth game. I'll settle for two hundred and ninety-nine."

Joe always replied, "Mose, you've earned three hundred a long time ago, and as long as you want to keep after it, I'll keep giving you a chance."

Finally, on July 25 in Boston, the old left-hander found a reserve of stuff and strength in his aging arm. While his teammates slammed base hits all over Fenway Park, he managed to stagger six innings to remain in front. He left the game when he couldn't pitch any longer, but he didn't have to. The Red Sox won by a big score and Grove had his precious three-hundredth victory. The old master celebrated by throwing a party for his teammates that night, and he didn't start another game. He retired with exactly three-hundred wins to his credit.

With the Yankees running away with the pennant and Grove's quest for immortality over, the attention of fans and experts was now directed toward the fabulous bat of Ted Williams. The major leagues hadn't had a .400 hitter since Bill Terry's .401 mark in 1930, and the last American League .400 hitter had been Harry Heilmann in 1923.

Nobody thought there would ever be another, especially when Williams fell to .399 on the last day of the season. The Red Sox were closing with a doubleheader against the

Athletics in Philadelphia, and everyone but Williams was concerned.

"Don't worry," he said before the game, "I'll make it all right."

He thereupon collected four hits in five trips to the plate in the first game to move up to .404.

"Ted," Joe told him in the locker room between games, "if you want to protect your average, it's all right with me. You don't have to play the second game."

"Yes, I do," Williams retorted. "If I'm a .400 hitter, it's for the whole season, not the season less one game."

Then he went out and got two more hits in three times at bat for a .406 average. The major leagues haven't seen a .400 hitter since.

Except for Williams's amazing performance, there was little for Joe to shout about until Mildred presented him with Michael Joseph, their second son, on July 6. From a baseball standpoint, 1941 was another year of disappointment for him. Late in the season, he hurt his arm, and Skeeter Newsome played short most of the time. Pytlak suddenly tired and Peacock couldn't do a consistently good job behind the plate, so Joe had to shuffle the team around. Foxx volunteered to catch, and since he had once been a receiver he did pretty well behind the plate. Lou Finney played first base. Tabor suddenly began to slip, which caused Joe to play third himself occasionally, although he used Hale part of the time.

In the batting category, the Red Sox hitting was not nearly as impressive as it had been in previous years. Joe, in and out of the line-up, batted .311, Pete Fox .302 and Jimmy Foxx .300. Otherwise, except, of course, for Williams, the club had no regulars batting .300 or more.

One bright spot was Dick Newsome's pitching performance. The big rookie won nineteen games, lost ten and

142

seemed to be facing a glittering future. Dobson, with a 12–5 won and lost mark, was disappointing but not hopelessly so, and Wagner and Hughson, the youngsters from the farm system, looked very promising.

As for Joe—he was ready to call it a career. The Red Sox had a fine young shortstop named Johnny Pesky in their farm system. "If Pesky makes it next year," Joe told Boston baseball writers, "I'll be a bench manager."

Although they led the league in batting for the third year in a row, the Red Sox finished seventeen games behind the league-leading Yankees. A margin that largely took away all the pleasure that might have been gained from second place. Joe was sick of being runner-up. He wanted to win.

But a new factor entered into the baseball picture with the Japanese attack on Pearl Harbor on December 7, 1941. The days of all younger stars were numbered. Sooner or later, the able-bodied would be called into the service. Things were so uncertain that, even after President Franklin D. Roosevelt gave the green light to the national game, nobody wanted to do much trading. Every team tried to keep the players it had, for there was no way of knowing when a decrepit old bench warmer might have to become a regular.

Yet the Red Sox team that Joe met in Sarasota in 1942 had not yet been riddled by wartime demands, and the problems he faced were much as they would have been had the war not been on. The draft had barely touched baseball at this point, although before the year was over, dozens of young ballplayers would be changing uniforms.

The first Red Sox regular to go was Frank Pytlak, who enlisted in the Navy in April. That left the catching up to Peacock and Bill Conroy, whom the Red Sox had bought from Oakland in the Pacific Coast League at the end of the

1941 season. With the exception of Pytlak, the club went through the 1942 campaign without losing a first-stringer.

The reality that Jimmy Foxx was now through had to be dealt with, and he was sold to the Chicago Cubs in June. The Red Sox had to use Tony Lupien, a rookie, at first base. Doerr was still at second and Tabor at third, with Pesky at short and Williams, DiMaggio and Pete Fox in the outfield.

It wasn't a bad season, but the outcome was in the same old familiar pattern. The Yankees moved out in front early in the season and stayed there. The Red Sox moved into second place and never got out. When the year was over, they were nine games behind, runners-up to the perennial American League champions for the fourth time in five years.

They had to be content with individual records again. Williams won the triple crown, leading the league in batting, home runs and runs batted in. Pesky not only did a fine job in his rookie season at short, but led the league in hits, with two hundred and five. And while Dick Newsome was disappointing, Tex Hughson blossomed into a star, winning twenty-two games to lead the league in that respect.

Joe played very little that year, filling in for injured infielders and using himself in a pinch-hitting capacity. He came through with key hits several times, and when the season was over, Eddie Collins remarked, "I think you'd better plan to play yourself more regularly next year. You can still hit."

"I can't move around the way I used to," Joe pointed out, "but if I'm needed I'll be in there somewhere."

At the end of the season, the boys started joining the colors. Williams and Pesky became Navy flight cadets, with Williams eventually becoming a Marine pilot. DiMaggio and Wagner joined the Navy. Youngsters in the farm system were being called up, and the minors in general all but disintegrated.

144

Travel restrictions were slapped on everywhere. The days of Florida training were over for the duration. So, too, were the days of private cars and special trains. Ballplayers made what trains they could in going from place to place, while traveling secretaries went out of their minds trying to keep track of them.

In the meantime, Joe did what he could to keep the Red Sox together. Everything was temporary, nothing stable. Baseball itself was alive only because the President sanctioned it; with far more serious cares on their minds, however, the fans couldn't get excited about the fortunes of their favorite ball clubs.

They were interested, of course, and came out to watch their teams in action. As always, Joe wanted to give the Boston fans the best team he could get together, but with Williams, Pesky, DiMaggio, Pytlak and Wagner gone, he knew he couldn't do much. Even with the club at full strength, the Red Sox hadn't been able to beat the Yankees. Now, with only half a team, they didn't have a chance.

Tom Yawkey told Joe before the beginning of the 1943 season, "Don't worry about anything—where we finish, how we do—or anything else. Your job is to keep baseball going, and if we win, so much the better. But if we lose, forget it."

"We'll forget it for now, Tom," Joe replied, "but when the war is over, we'll go after them again."

And it was with this attitude that Joe met his ballplayers for spring training in 1943, not at Sarasota, Florida, but at the Tufts College baseball cage in the Boston suburb of Medford, Massachusetts.

18.

With so many of the regulars gone, the 1943 team fell apart completely, and finished seventh. Their leading batter was Pete Fox, who hit .288, their leading home run hitter Bobby Doerr, with 16. The team as a whole averaged .244 at the plate, dropping from first to seventh in that respect. Except for Hughson, who won twelve games, and Oscar Judd, who had eleven, the other pitchers won nine games or less.

There was one redeeming feature of this horrible season, one burst of fireworks, and they were provided by Joe himself. As Collins had pointed out, he could still hit, and he didn't hesitate to put himself in as a pinch hitter when the need arose. In mid-June he began a remarkable streak which has never been matched before or since.

On June 15, the Athletics were murdering the Red Sox, 7–0, in the first game of a doubleheader at Fenway Park. The Red Sox got a rally going in the eighth inning when Roy Partee hit a single and Skeeter Newsome sent him to third with a double, bringing up the pitcher Mace Brown.

The time had come for a pinch hitter and Joe came up to face Lum Harris, the Philadelphia pitcher.

He fouled off the first one and watched the second go by for a ball. Then, with the count one and one, Harris threw a fast ball and Joe creamed it. The ball landed high in the screen atop the left field fence for a three-run homer to keep the Red Sox from being shut out, although they lost the game.

Two days later, the Athletics had a 4–1 lead, and Russ Christopher, their pitcher, seemed on his way to an easy victory when the Red Sox started some action in the eighth inning of the first game of another twin bill. Successive singles by Babe Barna and Skeeter Newsome put two men on with two out and the pitcher, Lou Lucier, due to bat.

Once again, Joe put himself in to pinch-hit. He watched a called ball go by, then smacked the second pitch over the left field fence for a three-run homer that tied the score. The Red Sox went on to win the game, 5–4, in the ninth.

The Athletics were in front by four runs in the eighth inning of the second game when Joe batted for Mike Ryba, the pitcher, with Doerr on second base and Newsome on first with two out. Don Black, the Athletics' hurler, worked carefully on Joe until the count ran to three balls and two strikes.

Then Black threw a fast ball across the inside corner, and Joe belted it to left field. The ball hugged the foul line but stayed fair. When it landed in the screen, Joe had his second pinch homer of the day, the only time anyone has ever hit home runs as a pinch hitter in each game of a doubleheader.

About a month later, on July 9, the Red Sox were losing to the Browns in St. Louis by a 4–2 score; Bill Conroy, the Red Sox catcher, was due up with one man on base and two out in the eighth inning. Joe yanked Conroy and went to the plate himself.

Bob Muncrief, the Browns' pitcher, threw two good pitches, one of which Joe fouled off, while the other went by for a called strike. Then the St. Louis right-hander tried to slip a curve ball past him. Joe saw it coming, hit it squarely as it started to break and smashed the ball into the left field bleachers to tie the score. The fact that the Browns won the game in the ninth was incidental, for it was Joe's fourth pinch homer of the year, tying the major league record.

Another month went by and the Red Sox, floundering around near the league cellar, went into Chicago for a doubleheader. Lee Rose was trying to protect a 4–1 White Sox lead when the Red Sox got two men on base with their pitcher George Woods slated to come to bat with one out in the seventh inning.

This time, after Joe inserted himself as a pinch hitter, he belted the first pitch, a high, screaming line drive which carried into the left field stands for a three-run homer to tie the score. The game went fourteen innings before the White Sox finally won, 7–6.

That smash gave Joe undisputed title to the all-time record for pinch homers for one year. His mark of five for the 1943 season has never been equaled.

The Boston club had been hit harder than any other American League team after the 1942 season was over, but the situation leveled off for them in 1943, while other teams were depleted by their stars going into service. So in 1944 the Red Sox were better able to cope with the other teams in the league.

But the Red Sox still weren't good enough to win the pennant, even in this worst of the war years. Once again they trained at Tufts College in Medford, for traveling was

148

cut to a minimum. This was a break for Joe, because he was home when Mildred gave birth to Maureen, their third child and first daughter, on April 30.

Service demands once more began decimating the ball club before the season was over. In May the Red Sox obtained catcher Hal Wagner from the Athletics, and he joined the Navy two months later. Tex Hughson went into the Army in August and Doerr, who came within two points of leading the league in batting, was called up in September. Others who were gone before the year was out were Roy Partee, Bill Conroy and Jim Tabor.

The second of Cronin's two five-year contracts was due to expire in October, but Tom Yawkey didn't wait that long to give him a new one. The Red Sox owner walked casually into Joe's office one day in August and remarked, "I've got your new contract. Come in and sign it any time."

This one, again calling for a raise in salary, was for three years instead of five. "Who knows what's going to happen?" Yawkey asked. "By 1947 we can work out something else, but I don't want you working without a contract in the meantime."

The Red Sox finished fourth in 1944, behind St. Louis, Detroit and New York. It was the only time the Browns, usually the doormats of the league, ever won the pennant. Joe got into seventy-six games, playing first base about a third of the season and using himself as a pinch hitter the rest of the time. He broke no records at the plate that year, but he still remained the only reliable clutch hitter on the ball club.

The Red Sox arranged to train in Atlantic City the following spring, where there was more chance of getting outdoors than in Medford. By that time, the end of the war was in sight and travel restrictions had been relaxed, although not

149

enough to permit their traveling all the way to Florida for spring training.

Every team in the major leagues had a nondescript collection of athletes on its roster, but the Red Sox group was worse than most. Only a few members of the squad which Cronin took to Atlantic City in 1945 were still with the club a year later when the veterans returned. The team was so bad that even Joe, who hated the thought, was almost resigned to finishing in the cellar, or, at best, in seventh place.

The ball club got off to a poor start, losing all three games of its opening series to the Yankees in New York. Joe, at first base, was nearly thirty-nine years old, overweight and slow, his reflexes gone. The intense desire to win was the only thing he had left.

On the third day of the 1945 season, while trying to beat out an infield hit in the first inning of a game in New York, Joe crashed into Nick Etten, the Yankee first baseman, and, as he went down, his right leg buckled under him. He had to be carried off the field with a broken leg. It was his last appearance in a major league ball game.

He was in the hospital for several days and couldn't rejoin the ball club for a couple of weeks after that. In the meantime, coach Del Baker took charge, and found it a rough assignment. The Red Sox lost one game after another, dropping their first eight. Joe was ready to write off the year completely.

But there was one glimmer of hope. In that season of 1945, the most valuable piece of baseball property was the ballplayer who had been discharged from the service, no matter what his age or physical condition. Cronin and Eddie Collins were both keeping a sharp eye out for any such men who might be available to them.

Checking over the line scores of exhibition games in the morning papers, just before the 1945 season began, Joe noticed that Dave (Boo) Ferriss had pitched a few innings for Louisville against the Cincinnati Reds. Louisville was a Red Sox farm club and Ferriss a big right-handed pitcher who had gone into the service in 1942. Further investigation disclosed that he had just been discharged from the Army Air Force because of asthma. When Joe found that out, he phoned Bill McKechnie, the Reds' manager, and asked, "How did Ferriss look in that game against you yesterday?"

"Not bad," McKechnie replied. "He's pretty green, but I wouldn't be surprised if he could help you."

Joe decided to wait a few days. In the meantime, he suffered the leg break and the Red Sox went into their nose dive. Before he rejoined the team, Joe came to the conclusion that even a green kid with only one year of organized ball under his belt might do better than some of the pitchers the Red Sox were using. He wired Louisville to send Ferriss to Philadelphia, where the club was opening a series with the Athletics.

By the time Ferriss reported, Del Baker, still running the Red Sox in Joe's absence, was desperate. The club had eight defeats, no victories and, so far as he could figure out, no pitchers who could do anything about it. Against his better judgment—for Baker was a conservative man who didn't believe in taking unnecessary chances—he sent Ferriss in to start the second game of the series in Philadelphia.

While Baker shuddered in the dugout, Ferriss, scared to death in his first big league appearance, threw eleven straight called balls, putting the first two men he faced on base and running the count to three balls and no strikes on the third man. But he got the twelfth pitch over, and the batter hit into a double play.

This set the pattern for the ball game. In one inning after another, the big rookie spent half his time getting into trouble and the other half getting out. He put men on bases in every inning, yet slammed the door when the Athletics threatened to score, ending up winning a shutout victory over them.

After that, to Joe's delight, Ferriss piled up an amazing series of records. He became the first rookie pitcher to beat every team in the league the first time he faced them. He won his first eight games, then, after losing one, took the next eight. Before the first of August, Ferriss had sixteen victories and only one defeat. The big, friendly twenty-three-year-old from Mississippi was the sensation of the league. He slipped in August when the pollen season aggravated his asthma, but he still won twenty-one games. He also hit seven doubles, a triple and a home run, and batted in nineteen runs.

The war ended in August, but it was too late to affect the baseball pennant races. Thanks to Ferriss, the Red Sox had climbed out of last place, but they slipped late in the season and finished seventh.

When it was all over, Joe sat down with Tom Yawkey and Eddie Collins to talk over plans for 1946. Collins, plagued by poor health, was finding it harder and harder to come in every day, and no longer was able to travel around the circuit or go off on scouting trips as he had in the past. As a result, Joe, almost without thinking about it, was assuming more responsibility than he ever had.

"What do you think we're going to need next year?" Yawkey asked him.

"A right-handed, long-hitting first baseman," Joe replied. "That's our first consideration. I think we ought to keep our eyes open for a third baseman, too, and we could use a solid right fielder."

The Red Sox still hadn't found a replacement for Foxx. Lupien, a left-handed hitter and not a very robust one at that, had been released. There was no one in the farm system who could fill the bill. The only hope the Red Sox had would be to make a deal.

"Who can we spare and who can spare us what we need?" Joe asked. It was a rhetorical question, one that could be answered only by going thoroughly over their roster and the rosters of the other clubs in the league.

"The trouble is," Joe pointed out, "most of the ballplayers we had this year are practically worthless on the open market. We have to give up a man who can be a big leaguer in real big league company, not wartime company."

"And we can't give up any of our big guys," Collins added. "Or any of the kids who looked promising in the minors. I think we ought to test them out before we let any of them go."

"You're right," Joe said. "But I'll tell you this—we'll get along all right without a new third baseman or right fielder, because we've got plenty of power and three or four guys who could fill in at those positions. But we've *got* to have that right-handed first baseman. He'll be the difference between winning and not winning a pennant."

A close roster check of other teams uncovered the man the Red Sox were looking for—Rudy York of the Detroit Tigers. The thirty-three-year-old slugger had had a poor season in 1945, batting .264 and hitting only eighteen home runs. The Tiger fans, toughest in the league, had been on him all year, and he would undoubtedly be glad to get out of Detroit. More important, Hank Greenberg, the team's regular first baseman, was returning, so the Tigers could spare York.

"York may have one good year left," Joe commented. "I'm going after him."

The next question was, "Who do we have that the Tigers can use?"

That wasn't hard to answer. Even though they had just

153

won the 1945 pennant, the Tigers needed a shortstop. Skeeter Webb, the son-in-law of the manager, Steve O'Neill, had played there all year, but he was a second baseman who had shifted over to fill the gap.

With Pesky returning, the Red Sox were set at shortstop and could give up Eddie Lake, one of the few real big leaguers who had played for them in 1945. When Joe left for the World Series in Detroit, he had the approval of both Yawkey and Collins to close the deal if he could.

He sat down with O'Neill on the night of the first World Series game and asked casually, "What are you going to do for a shortstop next year?"

O'Neill looked sharply at him, then answered the question with a question. "Have you got anyone in mind?" he asked.

"We can spare Lake," Joe said.

"Who do you want for him?"

"Rudy York."

"Let me think about it," the Detroit manager said.

The deal was made the next day. When he called Yawkey to tell him about it, Joe exclaimed, "Tom, this will give us that pennant we've been chasing all these years!"

"I sure hope you're right," his boss replied.

19.

With all clubs at full strength in 1946, baseball experts almost unanimously picked the Yankees to win and the Red Sox to finish second. But when Joe saw his reunited ball club in action at Sarasota a few times, he was convinced that at last he had a team that could give Tom Yawkey that ever-elusive pennant.

Practically all of the Red Sox were out of the service in time to report to Florida. Williams, DiMaggio and Hughson were discharged in January, Pesky and Doerr a month earlier. Hal Wagner and Mickey Harris had returned to civilian life in October, and Joe Dobson got out just in time to meet the team at the start of spring training. Every one of these men was essential in the master plan which Cronin had drawn.

There were still a few questions in his mind. One was answered before the end of spring training—what could be expected of Ferriss against bona fide big league competition? The big, soft-spoken right-hander looked as good in exhibition games as he had the previous summer and Joe knew he could be counted on.

As the team went north, Cronin was able to answer some of the other questions that had been bothering him. With York at first, Doerr at second and Pesky at short, three-quarters of the infield was set. Williams and DiMaggio would take care of two-thirds of the outfield. Wagner would do the bulk of the catching, and Roy Partee, who was getting out of the Army in a few weeks, would be available to help behind the bat.

The only questionable spots were third base and right field. The Red Sox had given up on Tabor. Joe was going to start the season with Eddie Pellagrini, a rookie, at third base; he also had Rip Russell and Leon Culberson, one of the few holdovers from the 1945 team. Right field would be split up between two other holdovers, George Metkovich and Tom McBride.

"I think we'll probably get by at third base," Joe told Eddie Collins, "but I'd be a lot happier if we could find a solid, experienced ballplayer."

The season started out as a scramble among the Red Sox, Yankees, Tigers and Indians, but it didn't remain that way for very long. On April 28, the Red Sox beat the Yankees in Boston and took undisputed possession of first place. They then went on a fifteen-game winning streak, following that with another twelve victories in a row. By then, Joe Cronin's men had made a shambles of the pennant race. They were so far ahead that nobody had a chance to catch them unless they fell flat on their faces.

It was a most remarkable season, one of the best ever enjoyed by a big league team. Everyone fit exactly into the place Joe had planned. Hughson, Ferris, Harris and Dobson all had great years, with Ferriss winning twenty-five games and Hughson twenty. Earl Johnson was the best relief pitcher of the year, and he had help from Bob Klinger, whom the Red Sox picked up in May after the Pirates had released him. In June they bought Bill Zuber from the Yankees, and he was good for spots. So was Bagby, who both started and relieved.

Almost all the others on the team had great years. Williams hit thirty-eight homers, drove in one hundred and twenty-three runs and batted .342, losing the title by a whisker to Mickey Vernon of the Senators. Pesky batted .335 and had two hundred and eight hits, his second straight season with more than two hundred. Doerr was the best second baseman in the league, with eighteen homers to boot. DiMaggio hit .316 and was such a flawless outfielder that Boston fans were singing "Who's better than his brother Joe? Dominic DiMaggio," to the tune of "Maryland, My Maryland" before the season was half over.

Just as Joe had hoped, York had one more great season left. He socked seventeen home runs, batted in 119 runs and was the perfect right-handed slugging first baseman to follow Williams in the batting order. Wagner did a good job of receiving and the two right fielders, Metkovich and McBride, were adequate.

There were only a few stumbling blocks, and they weren't serious enough to worry about. Joe had to keep shuffling his third basemen around, using seven by the time the season ended. He finally settled on Mike Higgins, whom the Red Sox bought back from Detroit. Higgins couldn't play every day, but was good for several days at a time, and his right-handed hitting came in very handy.

In midseason, Ted Williams ran into an unexpected problem. The Red Sox star had been ripping all pitching apart, and opposing managers were frantic trying to figure out ways to stop him. Lou Boudreau of the Indians finally came up with a radical shift. He packed the right side of the diamond, giving Williams all of the left.

When Cronin first saw this shift, he said to Williams, "Ted,

157

push the ball to left and Boudreau will have to put all those guys back where they belong."

"The heck I will," Williams retorted. "All my power is toward right, and I'll jam the ball through them."

He then went to the plate and hit a hot ground ball through what ordinarily would have been the hole between first base and second. Instead of going through as a single, it was fielded by Joe Gordon, the second baseman, playing far over toward first base, and Williams was thrown out. This happened again before the day was over, and it looked as if the Cleveland manager had solved the Williams problem.

In the locker room after the game, Joe spoke to his star again. "Ted," he said earnestly, "you were robbed of two hits today because you wouldn't hit to left field. Before you know it, every club in the league will be playing you this way."

"Let 'em," Williams growled. "They're not going to make me change my swing."

"All you have to do is place a ball to left once in a while," Cronin insisted. "Just let 'em know that they can't get away with this sort of thing."

"No, sir," Williams snapped. "I'm a pull hitter and I'll keep pulling, no matter how many guys they put over there."

News of Boudreau's shift spread like wildfire, and eventually every team was using it or a close variation whenever Williams came to the plate. Day after day, Joe pleaded and argued with him to hit to left, but except for one or two occasions Williams stubbornly refused. Baseball experts estimated that his insistence on hitting to right cost him thirty or forty points and the league batting title.

The Red Sox went further and further ahead of the pack. By mid-June they had lost only nine games and seemed on their way to all-time victory records. They tailed off in

August, however, but were still sixteen and a half games ahead of the second-place Tigers by Labor Day.

Then, needing only the combination of one victory and a Tiger defeat to clinch the pennant, they suddenly went into a tailspin. They lost a game in Washington, two more in Philadelphia, two more in Detroit and one in Cleveland, while the Tigers went through the same period without losing a game. By September 13, the Red Sox were just where they had been the week before—one game away from clinching the pennant. Now, however, they were only eleven and a half ahead of the Tigers.

"Come on," Joe cried in the locker room of League Park, Cleveland's old ball park. "This business has gone far enough. Let's get this thing clinched!"

He sent Tex Hughson in to pitch against Cleveland's Red Embree. In the first half of the first inning, Williams went to bat with two out and nobody on base. As usual, the Indians had the right side of the field packed against him. The only man on the other side was Pat Seerey, the Indians' rotund left fielder, in so close that he was practically playing a deep shortstop.

Williams watched one pitch go by, then, as the next came in, he suddenly shifted his stance and placed the ball over Seerey's head into left field. It rolled to the fence, and by the time the heavy-footed Cleveland outfielder retrieved it, Williams had gone all the way around the bases for an inside-the-park home run.

Except for a single by Johnny Pesky, the Red Sox didn't get another hit off Embree. But Hughson pitched a three-hit shutout, and the Red Sox won a 1–0 victory.

The Boston club still hadn't clinched the pennant, for the Tigers had to be beaten. They were playing the Yankees in Detroit that afternoon, but the game hadn't even started when the Red Sox–Indians game was over. Detroit was an hour behind Cleveland in time; furthermore, Cleveland games began at one o'clock while Detroit games began at two, Detroit time, which was three, Cleveland time. The Red Sox had achieved their victory in less than two hours, the game ending before three o'clock. They had to wait all afternoon to find out whether or not they were the American League champions.

Joe DiMaggio hit a home run to whip the Tigers that day, and it was the only time in his life the Yankee star clinched a pennant for the Red Sox. Dom sent him a wire of thanks when it was over, and the Red Sox were in.

Joe Cronin heard the news in a hotel suite at Cleveland's Hotel Statler, where he was relaxing with Tom Yawkey and several Boston writers. When it was all over, Joe quietly accepted congratulations from everyone there.

Then he said, "That was the way I wanted to win—with Hughson pitching a three-hitter and Williams hitting a home run. That's the way it should be. I've put Hughson in the toughest spots I could find, and he's always come through. As for Ted—what can I say that hasn't been said already? The guy's in a class by himself."

Somebody asked Yawkey if he had anything to say. The Red Sox owner, who had spent four million dollars waiting for this day, just grinned and remarked, "Don't talk to me. Talk to Joe—he's the guy who won the pennant for us."

The Red Sox had won it with ridiculous ease. If it hadn't been for their September slump, they would almost surely have broken the record for victories by a pennant winner. As it was, they settled for one hundred and four, finishing twelve ahead of Detroit.

Boston fans were deliriously happy, for this was their first pennant in twenty-eight years. They scrambled wildly for World Series tickets, and thousands of orders had to be returned.

Joe took special satisfaction from the victory, for he knew that many Red Sox followers had written him off as a perpetual second-place manager. He had always said that he could win with good pitching, and now he had finally proved it.

Aside from that, he was delighted to win the pennant in his first full season as a bench manager, just as he had won his first pennant in his first year as a playing manager. On top of that, he became the first manager in the history of the American League to win pennants with two different clubs. Only Al Lopez, who first won with Cleveland and then with Chicago, has duplicated the stunt since.

With the pennant clinched so soon, the Red Sox had a long coast to the end of the season. The letdown didn't help them any, and when the World Series was further delayed by a National League pennant playoff between the St. Louis Cardinals and the Brooklyn Dodgers, the Red Sox decided to play a game against an all-star team of American Leaguers just to keep sharp.

It was a disastrous mistake, for Ted Williams was hit by a pitch that bruised his arm. This could well have cost the Red Sox the World Series that followed.

The Cardinals won the National League flag, and the series began in St. Louis. Johnson won the opener for the Red Sox in relief of Hughson, with York settling the game by belting a home run in the tenth inning. The Cardinals evened things in the second game and the teams went to Boston. York smashed a three-run homer in the first inning of the third game and Ferriss won an easy shutout victory, but the Cardinals evened the series again by winning the fourth contest. When Dobson beat them in the fifth game, the Red Sox went back to St. Louis hoping to clinch the series in one more game.

They couldn't do it in two. Harry Brecheen, who had

already beaten them in the second game, whipped them again in the sixth. When he did it a third time as a relief pitcher in the seventh game, after Enos Slaughter had scored the winning run all the way from first base on a single, the Series was all over.

Ted Williams was held to five singles, one a bunt. By keeping the ball close to his fists, the Cardinal pitchers, especially Brecheen, all but handcuffed him.

When the Series was over, Joe walked from man to man, patting backs here, shaking hands there and generally trying to cheer everyone up. Williams was heartbroken; so, too, was Johnny Pesky, who had held the ball for several precious seconds after taking a relay throw from the outfield while Slaughter was on his mad dash for the plate.

"Never mind, boys," Joe consoled them. "We'll get 'em next year."

He wasn't kidding. As the team broke up for the winter, Joe fully expected that the 1946 triumph was only the first of a long series of Red Sox pennants. He saw no reason why this shouldn't happen. Only a major disaster could stop the Red Sox from dominating the big league baseball scene for several years to come.

20.

EDDIE COLLINS WAS FAILING. THE RED SOX GENERAL MANAGER had a heart condition, and although he insisted on going to the 1946 World Series he was unable to travel much after that. The winter meetings were held in Los Angeles that year, and he couldn't make the long trip. Neither could Tom Yawkey, so Joe was the only high-ranking Red Sox official there.

He made no big deals and hadn't expected to. Other ball clubs sounded him out, but he flatly refused to part with any first-line ballplayers. Except for a few men bought and sold on waivers, he did very little business that year.

In the spring at Sarasota it appeared that the Red Sox suffered from an embarrassment of riches, especially in the pitching department. Besides the big four from the 1946 team, there were four more very promising rookies from the farm clubs. Tommy Fine had won twenty-three games for Scranton; Mel Parnell, a smooth southpaw, had had a sensational 1.30 earned-run average there; Harry Dorish and Al

Widmar had both done well at Louisville. It looked as if the Red Sox had more pitchers than they could possibly use.

In addition, Sam Mele, a rookie outfielder who had batted .342 for Scranton in 1946, appeared to be the man who would solve the right field problem. The only weakness was at third base, where Joe would have to do some maneuvering; the rest of the team seemed so powerful, however, that this didn't worry him.

Between their great 1946 season and the fine-looking collection of coming youngsters, the Red Sox were odds-on choices to romp to a 1947 pennant. Joe was as sure of it as anyone, and he went through most of the spring training season with high hopes for the campaign ahead.

Then Dave Ferriss came up with a sore arm.

"It only hurts a little," the big right-hander said. "I can live with it all right."

Joe assured him he could win with it, too, but he said it with his fingers crossed. He had counted on Ferriss for twenty games; now he didn't know what to expect. All Joe could do was hope the young man who had checked in with twenty-five games in 1946 hadn't lost his stuff.

Then, just before the season began, Mickey Harris' arm went bad. "It seems like it's dropping off," he told Win Green, the trainer. "I can hardly lift it."

"We'll work on it," Green said. "Maybe it'll be all right."

It wasn't. Harris started once or twice, but every pitch was agony. He had lost his fast ball, and without a fast ball, he was just another pitcher.

The crowning blow came a month after the season opened. Halfway through a ball game at Fenway Park, Tex Hughson felt a twinge in his arm. When Cronin went out from the dugout to talk to him, he moaned, "I don't know what's wrong with it, Joe. I've never had anything like this before."

"Don't pitch any more," Joe said. "We'll have somebody look at it."

Later, he told writers following the Red Sox, "If I hadn't seen it with my own eyes, I wouldn't believe it could happen. How can a ball club have three of its four top pitchers come up with sore arms, practically all at once?"

"What are you going to do, Joe?" someone asked him.

"Just hope for the best. I'll pitch the fellows when they feel like pitching, and when they don't I'll have to use somebody else. Before the season started, I'd have sworn the pennant was in." Then, shaking his head sadly, Cronin added, "Now, I don't know where we'll finish."

Of the rookie pitchers who had looked so promising in the spring, only Dorish turned out to be of any help that year. Parnell needed experience and went back to the minors. Widmar and Fine simply couldn't make it, and Joe finally gave up on both.

It was bad enough to be plagued with pitching problems, but Joe had other worries, too. The first base situation was desperate. Rudy York, having had his one great year, obviously wasn't going to have another. The catching left something to be desired. And the Red Sox were still weak at third base.

In May Joe traded Wagner to the Detroit Tigers for Birdie Tebbetts, a deal that turned out very well. Tebbetts was the smartest receiver in the league and, while not a robust hitter, occasionally rattled a ball off the left field fence or hit one over it. A month after Tebbetts joined the club, Joe traded York to the White Sox for a big right-handed first baseman named Jake Jones.

Jones got off to an auspicious start, slamming home runs in each game of a doubleheader the first day he played for the Red Sox. That was twice as many as he slammed all the rest of the season. Joe, who had hoped Jones would be the right-handed slugger he needed to follow Williams, discovered that the young man couldn't hit a curve ball.

The season progressed and the Red Sox staggered along around fourth place. They finally moved up to second, then dropped to third, where they finished. The Yankees won the pennant, with the Tigers coming in second for the second straight year.

Despite the disastrous season, the Red Sox had a few compensations. Ted Williams enjoyed another remarkable year. Even though he still refused to hit to left field, he won the triple crown, leading the league in batting, home runs and runs batted in. Johnny Pesky batted .324 and piled up more than two hundred hits for his third season in a row. Sam Mele filled the gap in right field and his .302 average was more than adequate for a rookie.

Cronin maneuvered pitchers around endlessly. He couldn't make plans more than a few hours in advance. Instead of designating hurlers in rotation, he had to ask them how they felt before sending them into action.

Joe Dobson saved the pitching staff from falling apart completely. The only one of the 1946 starters with a sound arm, he won eighteen games while losing eight. The other three had miserable seasons—Ferriss and Hughson both won twelve and lost eleven and Harris, who couldn't pitch at all for more than half the season, won five and lost four.

While Tebbetts closed up the hole behind the plate and Jones spent most of the season on first base, the third base situation was never resolved. Joe used six different men at third that year, none of whom played more than forty-six games at the position. He even shifted Pesky over from shortstop, replacing Johnny with Eddie Pellagrini, but that didn't work either.

The nightmare year ended at last. Just before the finish, Tom Yawkey walked into Joe's office, sat down and began a conversation which was to change the entire course of Cronin's career.

"Joe," the Red Sox owner commented, "I think it's time for you to come into the front office."

"I'd like to win another pennant as manager," Joe said. "And this time add a World Series victory."

"I'd like to see you do it," the other agreed, "but I need you up here. Eddie Collins is pretty sick, and he just can't handle the job of general manager any more. You've practically been that anyhow. Now I want you to concentrate on the job. We'll get a new field manager, and you'll run the whole works."

They discussed the situation for some time. As they talked, Joe realized that Yawkey was right. Collins' health prevented him from continuing to assume the responsibility he had held for nearly 15 years. The team had to have a new general manager, somebody who knew its problems, had ideas how to solve them and enjoyed Yawkey's trust. Joe fit the picture perfectly. Finally, to Yawkey's obvious delight, he accepted it.

Before that conference was over, the two had made several other important decisions. At Joe's suggestion, they decided to go after Joe McCarthy to run the team on the field. McCarthy had retired as the Yankees' manager in 1946, after having won eight pennants with them. He and Joe Cronin were close friends. Joe phoned him at his home outside Buffalo, and McCarthy, then recognized as the greatest manager in baseball history, accepted on the spot.

Joe and Yawkey also discussed the team's troubles. They agreed they had to seek solid pitching, a third baseman capable of playing all season, and a heavy-hitting right-

167

handed slugger to follow Williams in the batting order, preferably a first baseman like the Rudy York of 1946. They reserved judgment on Jake Jones. Joe hoped he might learn to hit a curve ball, in which case he would do.

The two men talked about everything except Joe's contract, which had just expired. In the years that followed, they never mentioned either it or Joe's salary. The three-year pact that he had signed as manager in 1944 was the last formal contract Joe ever had with Yawkey. From 1947 on, a handshake sufficed.

The announcement that Joe Cronin was the general manager and Joe McCarthy the field manager of the Red Sox hit baseball fans in general—and Boston fans in particular— like a bombshell. Except for a few newspapermen who had been tipped off by Yawkey, no one had the slightest idea that such a change was in the works; in fact, it later developed that the Red Sox owner had told veteran newspapermen about it before he told Cronin.

Even though the shift was a complete surprise to Joe, he took it in stride. As soon as the World Series was over, he began looking around for the men he knew McCarthy would need if the Red Sox were to win any more pennants. For the next few weeks, Joe burned up the long-distance telephone lines in search of his quarry.

He found what he needed in St. Louis. The Browns, after winning the wartime 1944 pennant, had sunk right back into the oblivion from which they had come. But they had some good ballplayers, and Joe was ready to offer as much as necessary in order to get them. Bill DeWitt, the Browns' general manager, drove a hard bargain, but he and Joe finally agreed to a series of deals so fantastic that it rivaled the trade in which Joe himself had been involved when he came to the Red Sox from Washington.

On successive days, Joe acquired Jack Kramer and Ellis Kinder, two front-line pitchers, Junior Stephens, a slugging right-handed shortstop, and Billy Hitchcock, a good utility infielder, for eight players and over four hundred thousand dollars in cash. Not one of the men given up by the Red Sox figured in their future plans.

Throughout the country, baseball writers agreed. "Cronin has bought a pennant for Yawkey," one proclaimed, summing it up for them all. There seemed little doubt that this was true.

Kramer and Kinder, both right-handers, were potential twenty-game winners. Stephens was the man to follow Williams in the batting order. At Fenway Park, the chunky shortstop, a great pull hitter, would murder opposing pitchers, who no longer could safely pass Williams purposely, as they had done all during the 1947 season. Hitchcock would fill in wherever he was needed, and would also be available for pinch-hitting duties. Some Boston writers wondered what would happen to Pesky, but McCarthy answered that by shifting him over to third base.

When the 1948 baseball season opened, the Red Sox were practically the unanimous choice to win the pennant going away. They got off to a terrible start, struggling along in the second division for nearly two months. But they made a strong finish to end up in a top tie with Cleveland, necessitating the first playoff in the history of the American League. The Indians won it, so the elusive pennant was again lost.

From his perch in the front office, Cronin died a thousand deaths, along with all the rest of the Red Sox fans. The loss was especially hard to take because the Braves, then in Boston, won the National League pennant, and there had been confident talk in Boston about a city World Series. When it didn't deveolp, the Red Sox were the goats, and an old cry, "What's the matter with the Red Sox?" swept the city.

Joe was the man expected to answer it. When writers and fans alike swamped him, he smiled calmly and replied, "Nothing. It's a great ball club—and I'm proud of it."

He had reason to make the same statement a hundred times during the next few years.

21.

IN THE YEARS THAT FOLLOWED JOE CRONIN'S APPOINTMENT as general manager of the Red Sox, while the team had its ups and downs, it never reached the heights to which Joe himself had led it. In 1949, McCarthy's second year as manager, the Red Sox again missed winning the pennant by a whisker. They lost to the Yankees on the very last day of the season. From then on, they began to slip.

The great team that Collins and Cronin had built up for Yawkey was creaking at the seams. The stars of the forties began aging in the fifties, and it was increasingly more difficult to find talented replacements. Joe built up a huge scouting system, but other teams were doing the same thing. The competition became keener every year, and although the Red Sox got their fair share of bonus boys, few of them developed.

Actually, the bad luck which hit so hard in 1947 with the folding of the pitching staff seemed to dog the Red Sox in the years that followed. Their top prospects, youngsters sought after by every other team in baseball, either got

171

hurt, quit too soon or simply didn't turn out to be as good as they had looked.

Despite criticism, Joe refused to panic. He had faith in the men he had appointed to run the farm system, and he realized better than any outsider that the failures were not the fault of the scouts.

"How can you blame scouts when a pitcher comes up with a sore arm?" he said, time and again. "Whose fault is it when a slugger breaks his leg and can't regain his swing after it's healed? I believe that luck and the breaks are as important as anything in this business. If you don't have either you run into trouble, because that's the nature of the game of baseball."

He was desperately anxious to rebuild a team that would bring gladness to the heart of the ever-patient Tom Yawkey. Yawkey gave Joe a blank check, told him to spend as much money as necessary to bring Boston another pennant, but now Joe knew that great teams could no longer be bought as in previous years. Everyone had money, everyone was looking for talent. Nobody was interested in selling ballplayers for cash any more.

A shrewd and cautious trader, Joe was highly respected all over the American League. One of the few ballplayers who ever moved into a top front office job, he had contacts wherever baseball was played. Men wanted to work for him, helped him and tipped him off whenever they could. Before he became the Red Sox general manager, Joe already had hundreds of friends. He made many more by the way he handled himself after he took over the job.

His kindness, his understanding, his patience and his interest in the welfare of others were genuine and sincere. Some people accused him of being ultraconservative, for Joe always preferred letting problems iron themselves out, but if a situation demanded action he was quite capable of making the proper move.

In 1952, for example, the Red Sox had an unusual puzzle in the case of Jimmy Piersall. The great outfielder was then a fiery rookie, so intense and so eager to make the grade that the pressure became too much for him, and he eventually needed medical attention. Joe was one of the first to recognize that Piersall's nervousness was caused by abnormal anxieties, and that the youngster suffered from a mental disturbance. Through his efforts, Piersall was hospitalized and given the care he needed to bring him back to reality. After Piersall was cured, Joe saw to it that the once-troubled young man and his family would be able to spend the winter in Florida at the expense of the Red Sox.

Joe's one weakness was that he might have been too kindhearted. He still found it almost impossible to fire anyone and difficult to punish recalcitrants. Always a believer in treating people with the same consideration he would want for himself, he sometimes found that this policy backfired. When others took advantage of his good nature, his reaction was more often disappointment than anger.

But he could crack down when he had to. He never hesitated to trade a ballplayer who refused to stay in training, and he once fined Ted Williams five thousand dollars for spitting in the direction of the fans. If the fine was later rescinded, it was by Yawkey, not Joe. Cronin was willing to put up with a great deal from Williams, but not open insults to fans. To Joe, the fans always came first.

Not that they were always fair to him. In the years when the team was just missing pennants, many blamed him for the failures. Later, after the Red Sox began to slip, these same fans yearned for the great clubs which Joe had been so instrumental in building. They appreciated by then that it was better to be fighting for the pennant than for a place

173

in the first division. At least the teams of the late thirties and forties had been interesting, exciting ball clubs, even if they won but one pennant.

Soon after he became general manager, Joe learned that his duties went beyond the confines of Fenway Park. He was asked to take part in community activities, and he began to win honors that had nothing to do with baseball.

He became a member of the Variety Club, which sponsored the Jimmy Fund. This campaign raised money for cancer research for children, and both Boston ball clubs were active in it. When the Braves moved to Milwaukee, the Red Sox took over full responsibility for baseball's share in the organization. Eventually Joe won the Variety Club's Great Heart Award for his part in building and maintaining the Jimmy Fund.

He was named a Knight of Malta, a Papal appointment reserved only for the world's most prominent Catholics. He and others founded the Massachusetts Committee of Catholics, Protestants and Jews, of which he is still a director. He took part in many community activities and was in great demand as a speaker at civic functions.

Despite his many years as manager of the Red Sox, Joe never really felt that he belonged permanently in Boston until after he became involved in outside activities. Then, when Kevin, his third son and fourth child, was born in 1950, he knew he was a Bostonian for life.

"I guess I always thought vaguely about returning to San Francisco someday," he told Mildred. "But now I never want to go back except for visits."

"This is our home," his wife replied simply. "I hope we stay here for good."

"We will if I have anything to say about it," he said.

In 1956, the Red Sox moved their Triple A farm club from Louisville to San Francisco, which then had a team in the Pacific Coast League. With nothing more to go on than that Cronin had once lived in San Francisco, a Boston writer declared that this was the first in a series of moves which would be climaxed with the transfer of the Red Sox there from Boston.

"Joe Cronin wants to go back to his home town," the reporter wrote. "Now that the Red Sox control the territory, he won't hesitate to move them there."

The rumor was so completely unfounded that Joe refused to dignify it by a denial. But privately he remarked to friends, "How ridiculous can you get? I've lived here for twenty years. My three youngest children were born here, and even Tommy, my oldest, never knew any other city but Boston as home. And even if I did want to move back to San Francisco—which I don't—the Red Sox aren't mine. They belong to Tom Yawkey. If he ever had ideas about moving the Red Sox—and I've never heard him express any—he would be the one to do it, not I."

Two years later, Joe helped to clear the way for the New York Giants to move to San Francisco by arranging the transfer of the territory to the Giants' organization, and the top Red Sox farm club was shifted to Minneapolis. That ended any further speculation about Joe's alleged desire to move to San Francisco.

One day late in January of 1956, Joe left Fenway Park for his home in Newton. It had been a busy day, climaxed by his announcement that the Red Sox had just given Mike Higgins a three-year contract as manager. After bidding good night to his office associates, Joe got into his car for the thirty-minute drive. As usual, he turned on the radio for the six o'clock news.

Just as he was pulling up to a red traffic light, he heard an electrifying announcement.

"Two of baseball's general managers," it said, "Joe Cronin

175

of the Boston Red Sox and Hank Greenberg of the Cleveland Indians, have just been elected to the game's Hall of Fame."

For a minute Joe could hardly believe his ears. He leaned forward, but the announcer had already moved to another subject.

The Hall of Fame!

He drove the rest of the way home on a pink cloud of delight. Over and over, his heart pounding, he repeated the magic words. And when he got home he couldn't wait to break the news to his family.

He didn't have to. By the time he arrived, they knew all about it.

"How could we help it?" one of the children said. "The phone keeps ringing and everybody wants to speak to *you.*"

Joe laughed and retorted, "I guess *your* calls will have to wait. It's not every day that a guy makes the Hall of Fame."

The first thing he did was wire congratulations to Greenberg, who was in the process of sending the same sort of wire to Joe at that very moment.

"I don't know of anybody I'd rather go in with than Hank," Joe commented later. "We're both poor kids from big cities who made it the hard way."

Then he added, "It's kind of unbelievable that I'm in the same company with people like Babe Ruth, Lou Gehrig, Rogers Hornsby and Paul Waner. Now—" Joe's blue eyes twinkled and his face relaxed into a warm grin "—I'm more convinced than ever that when I was hitting the ball, the wind must have been blowing out."

He spent the next few months answering wires and letters and phone calls, for it seemed that all the thousands of friends he had made wanted to let him know how happy they were for him. Then, on the night of July 20, a crowd of over thirty-two thousand fans gathered at Fenway Park to pay tribute to him before a night game.

Three days later, Joe headed for Cooperstown, New York, site of baseball's Hall of Fame, to attend his and Hank Greenberg's induction. As he and Mildred drove off, their car gleamed with a new Massachusetts license plate which had been made especially for him.

It read: "HF."

22.

THE LONGER CRONIN SERVED AS THE RED SOX GENERAL MAN-
ager, the more active he became in American League affairs.
This was quite natural, since his boss Tom Yawkey was vice-
president of the league and had been one of its directors
since 1944. Yawkey encouraged Joe to spend as much spare
time as possible on league business, and Joe held active
membership on most of its important committees.

The game's top echelon was the Executive Council, a five-
man group that included the baseball commissioner, the
presidents of the two major leagues and one representative
from each league. Yawkey had been the American League
representative for several years when he was elected vice-
president in 1956. Joe was named to succeed him on the
Executive Council, and from then on Joe had a hand in the
shaping of the policies of all phases of baseball.

The American League president was William Harridge,
who had first been elected in 1931 and re-elected in 1956
for a ten-year term. But Harridge, whose headquarters were
in Chicago, was finding the job increasingly more difficult

for a man of his years, and in 1958 he began talking of stepping down in favor of a younger man.

Joe was aware of Harridge's apparent intention to resign, but was too busy with Red Sox problems to give it more than a passing thought. The team was deep in troubles of its own. Ted Williams, the last of its great stars, was nearing the end of the trail, and the rebuilding job would take time. Although there were promising kids in the farm system, they weren't ready yet.

As optimistic as ever, Joe looked forward to the future with eager anticipation. "Give us about four years," he told his assistant Joe McKenney, "and we'll be fighting for the pennant again."

As always, he discussed problems on the long-distance telephone with Tom Yawkey, and was looking forward to seeing him at the 1958 winter meetings in Washington. During one of these conversations, Yawkey casually remarked, "Joe, it looks as if Harridge will announce his resignation very soon."

"I had heard he was thinking about it," Joe said.

"Some of the owners would like to see you replace him," Yawkey went on.

Joe laughed, then remarked, "That's very flattering, but I hardly think I'm qualified for it."

"I wouldn't say that, Joe," the Red Sox owner commented. "As a matter of fact, I've already told people who inquired that we wouldn't stand in your way if you were offered the job."

"That's very nice of you, Tom, and I appreciate it," Joe said. "But that's a bridge I won't cross until or unless I come to it."

He thought no more about it until December, when Harridge actually announced his resignation, effective on February 1, 1959. Then, in common with everyone else in the American League, Joe wondered about Harridge's successor, who would be chosen by the American League owners. Despite his talk with Yawkey, Joe couldn't believe that anyone was seriously considering him for the job.

But the night that he checked into the Statler-Hilton Hotel in Washington for the December meetings, a group of the club owners, including Dan Topping of the Yankees, Chuck Comiskey of the White Sox, Calvin Griffith of the Senators and Tom Yawkey, paid him a formal visit in his suite. These men made up a special steering committee to investigate and recommend candidates for the presidency of the American League.

"Will you accept the job if it's offered to you?" a spokesman asked Joe.

Joe turned to Yawkey. "What's your feeling about this?" he asked.

"I think you already know," Yawkey replied. "If you have a chance to become president of the American League, the Red Sox will be happy to release you from any obligation with them."

"Thank you very much." Joe said quietly. Then, turning to the others, he added, "Naturally, under the circumstances, I'll accept—if the league wants me."

Nothing more was done in Washington, but the word spread quickly that Joe was the most likely man to succeed Harridge, and the story broke in the nation's newspapers. However, Joe still had to face a screening committee of owners who would make the final choice, and he was asked to meet this group in Chicago on January 14, 1959.

As the date approached, Boston fans and newspapermen became more and more excited over the possibility that the man who had been star and manager, then general manager

180

of the Red Sox for nearly a quarter of a century might become the first former ballplayer ever to lead one of the two big leagues.

When it was time for Joe to leave for Chicago, four Boston baseball writers, Tom Monahan of the *Traveler*, Bob Holbrook of the *Globe*, Joe Cashman of the *Record* and Arthur Sampson of the *Herald*, accompanied him. Also in the group were Joe McKenney, who had agreed to join Joe in the American League office if he got the job, and Jack Hayes, the Red Sox attorney, who was to represent Yawkey at the Chicago meeting.

"Whatever happens," Joe told them as their train pulled into Chicago, "I want all you fellows to be my guests at dinner tonight."

They checked into the Conrad Hilton Hotel. That afternoon they proceeded to the Palmer House for Cronin's meeting with the screening committee. Just before he entered the room, Joe turned to the others and said, "Don't forget—dinner tonight in my suite." Then he disappeared through the door.

The rest was automatic. Joe was the only candidate. He was swiftly elected the fourth president of the American League, and given a seven-year contract at an annual salary of sixty thousand dollars. The moment the announcement was made, phone calls and wires began pouring in. Once again, the thousands of friends, big and little, whom Joe had made down through the years were as happy for him as he was for himself.

His first move was to call Mildred at home in Newton. His next was to announce that Joe McKenney would be the league's director of public relations and his principal assistant. He was busy for the rest of the afternoon acknowledging congratulations and refusing countless invitations for dinner.

"I'm tied up tonight," he said over and over.

He spent that evening hosting his dinner party for the Boston group that had accompanied him to Chicago. He has taken the same group to dinner on January 14 every year since.

After he arrived home, the new president of the American League was asked if he intended to move to Chicago, where the league headquarters had been for nearly sixty years.

"No," he replied, "I'm not moving to Chicago or anywhere else. I'm setting up our headquarters right here in Boston. This is my home and this is where I intend to stay."

On February 1, Joe Cronin, the kid who grew up on the sandlots of San Francisco to become big league ballplayer, star, Most Valuable Player, manager, pennant winner, All-Star game hero, general manager and Hall of Famer, became president of the American League.

When Hank Greenberg, his Hall of Fame partner, remarked, "I can't think of anyone who deserves it more," there wasn't a single dissenting voice.

JOSEPH EDWARD CRONIN
Born: October 12, 1906

Batted right, threw right

Height: 6 ft.
Weight: 187 lbs.

Year Club	League	Pos.	G.	AB.	R.	H.	2B.	3B.	HR.	RBI.	B.A.	PO.	A.	E.	F.A.
1925 Johnstown	Mid.-Atl.	SS	99	352	64	110	18	11	3	—	.313	—	—	—	—
1926 Pittsburgh	Nat.	2B-SS	38	83	9	22	2	2	0	11	.265	74	92	6	.965
1926 New Haven	East.	SS	66	244	61	78	11	8	2	—	.320	136	222	27	.930
1927 Pittsburgh	Nat.	SS	12	22	2	5	1	0	0	3	.227	28	31	3	.952
1928 Kansas City	A.A.	3B-SS	74	241	34	59	10	6	2	32	.245	87	146	14	.943
1928 Washington	Amer.	SS	63	227	23	55	10	4	0	25	.243	133	190	16	.953
1929 Washington	Amer.	SS	145	492	72	139	29	8	8	60	.282	285	459	62	.923
1930 Washington	Amer.	SS	154	587	127	203	41	8	13	126	.346	336	509	35	.960
1931 Washington	Amer.	SS	156	611	103	187	44	13	12	126	.306	323	488	43	.950
1932 Washington	Amer.	SS	143	557	95	177	43	18	6	116	.318	306	448	32	.959
1933 Washington	Amer.	SS	152	602	89	186	45	11	5	118	.309	297	528	34	.960
1934 Washington	Amer.	SS	127	504	68	143	30	9	7	101	.284	246	486	38	.951
1935 Boston	Amer.	1B-SS	144	556	70	164	37	14	9	95	.295	277	435	37	.951
1936 Boston	Amer.	SS-3B	81	295	36	83	22	4	2	43	.281	133	229	26	.933
1937 Boston	Amer.	SS	148	570	102	175	40	4	18	110	.307	300	414	31	.958
1938 Boston	Amer.	SS	143	530	98	172	51	5	17	94	.325	304	499	36	.954
1939 Boston	Amer.	SS	143	520	97	160	33	3	19	107	.308	306	437	32	.959
1940 Boston	Amer.	3B-SS	149	548	104	156	35	6	24	111	.285	253	445	38	.948
1941 Boston	Amer.	SS-3B-OF	143	518	98	161	38	8	16	95	.311	247	362	27	.958
1942 Boston	Amer.	1B-3B-SS	45	79	7	24	3	0	4	24	.304	47	28	6	.926
1943 Boston	Amer.	3B-PH	59	77	8	24	4	0	5	29	.312	12	18	1	.968
1944 Boston	Amer.	1B-PH	76	191	24	46	7	0	5	28	.241	428	27	9	.981
1945 Boston	Amer.	3B	3	8	1	3	0	0	0	1	.375	2	8	0	1.000
Major League totals			2124	7577	1233	2285	515	117	171	1423	.302	4337	6083	512	.953

WORLD SERIES RECORD

Year Club	League	Pos.	G.	AB.	R.	H.	2B.	3B.	HR.	RBI.	B.A.	PO.	A.	E.	F.A.
1933 Washington	Amer.	SS	5	22	1	7	0	0	0	2	.318	7	15	1	.957

INDEX

187

Goslin, Goose, 67, 76-78, 84, 94, 100
Graham, Charlie, 21, 29-30
Grantham, George, 38
Gray, Sam, 61, 63
Green, Win, 164
Greenberg, Hank, 153, 176, 182
Griffith, Calvin, 180
Griffith, Clark, 9-16, 19, 49, 51, 52-53, 55, 58, 73-79, 81, 97-98, 99, 102-03, 104-05, 107
Griffith Stadium, 84, 89, 92
Grove, Lefty, 62, 63-64, 106, 108-09, 111-12, 115-16, 119, 124, 125, 126, 128, 131, 135, 137, 139, 140-41

Hadley, Bump, 62
Hagar, Philomena, 36
Hall of Fame, 176-77
Hale, Sammy, 111, 139, 142
Harder, Mel, 72
Harridge, William, 178-80
Harris, Bucky, 13, 52-53, 55, 56, 73, 75, 106
Harris, Dave, 101
Harris, Elmer, 22
Harris, Joe, 44-45
Harris, Lum, 147
Harris, Mickey, 155, 164
Harris, Stella, 20-21
Hauser, Joe, 45
Hayes, Jack, 181
Heilmann, Harry, 141
Heving, Joe, 128, 131
Higgins, Mike, 115, 118-19, 124, 130-31, 157, 175
Hitchcock, Billy, 169
Holbrook, Bob, 181
Hornsby, Rogers, 176
Hoyt, Waite, 54
Hubbell, Carl, 94, 95, 101
Hughes, Roy, 111

Hughson, Tex, 140, 143, 144, 146, 149, 155, 156, 159, 161, 164, 166

Indians, Cleveland. *See* Cleveland Indians
Ireland, 18

Jackson, Travis, 85
Jimmy Fund, 174
Johnson, Earl, 156, 161
Johnson, Roy, 107, 112
Johnson, Walter, 56, 58, 59, 66, 70-73, 81-82
Johnstown baseball club, 34-35, 46
Jones, Jake, 165-66, 168
Jones, Sam, 62
Judd, Oscar, 146
Judge, Joe, 53, 59

Kansas City Blues, 44-48
Kerr, Johnny, 86, 90
Kimsey, Chad, 63, 90
Kinder, Ellis, 169
Klinger, Bob, 156
Knickerbocker, Billy, 111
Knight of Malta, 174
Kramer, Jack, 169
Kress, Red, 101
Kuhel, Joe, 59, 77, 84, 95, 96, 100

Lake, Eddie, 154
Lary, Lyn, 15-16
Lazzeri, Tony, 43, 85, 88
Linke, Ed, 101
Lom, Benny, 22
Lopez, Al, 161
Los Angeles, California, 163
Louisville baseball club, 46, 48, 151, 164, 174
Lucier, Lou, 147
Luque, Dolf, 96
Lupien, Tony, 144, 152

188

McBride, George, 73
McBride, Tom, 156-57
McCarey, Socko, 42-43
McCarthy, Joe, 85, 124, 167-68, 169, 171
McGowan, Frank, 46, 48
McGraw, John, 93
McKain, Arch, 126-27, 130
McKechnie, Bill, 33, 36, 38, 41, 151
McKenney, Joe, 179, 181
McNair, Eric, 112-13, 118, 119, 122
Mack, Connie, 83, 106, 112
Madigan, Slip, 25-26, 30
Mancuso, Gus, 95, 96
Manush, Heine, 67, 84, 87-88, 92, 96, 100, 112-13, 119
Marberry, Firpo, 77-78
Marcum, Johnny, 112-13, 115, 119
Martin, Mike, 70-71, 90
Massachusetts, 174, 177
Massachusetts Committee of Catholics, Protestants and Jews, 174
Medford, Massachusetts, 145, 148
Mele, Sam, 164, 166
Melillo, Oscar, 92, 109
Metkovich, George, 156-57
Meusel, Bob, 43, 54
Milan, Clyde, 73
Miller, Bing, 107
Millers, Minneapolis. *See* Minneapolis Millers
Milwaukee, Wisconsin, 174
Minneapolis Millers, 45, 123, 130, 175
Mission High School, 22
Monahan, Tom, 181
Montague, Eddie, 32-36, 43-44
Moore, Eddie, 38
Moore, Joe, 94
Moore, Wilcy, 54

Muncrief, Bob, 148
Myatt, George, 116-17
Myer, Buddy, 59, 84, 85-86, 87, 90, 94, 100

Napa baseball club, 26-28
New Haven baseball team, 37-38, 46
New York City, 62, 76-78, 94, 132
New York Giants, 52, 93-96, 175
New York Yankees, 18, 43, 53-55, 60, 62, 68, 70, 72, 85-86, 87-88, 91, 92, 105, 108, 109, 110, 124-28, 132-35, 138, 149, 150, 156, 166, 171
Newsom, Buck, 119, 121
Newsome, Dick, 140, 142-43, 144
Newsome, Skeeter, 139, 141, 146-47
Newton, Massachusetts, 136, 175

Oakland Roofers, 36
O'Doul, Lefty, 98
Oliver, Tom, 61
O'Neill, Steve, 154
Ostermueller, Fritz, 116, 125, 128, 131, 133
Ott, Mel, 94, 96

Pacific Coast League, 116, 136, 140, 143, 174
Parnell, Mel, 163, 165
Partee, Roy, 146, 149, 156
Paso Robles, California, 32, 36, 44
Payne Field, 122
Peacock, Johnny, 131, 142, 143
Pearson, Monte, 133-34
Peckinpaugh, Roger, 52
Pellagrini, Eddie, 156, 166
Pesky, Johnny, 143, 144, 155-57, 159, 162, 166, 169
Phelan, Tom, 27-28

189

191

About the Author

AL HIRSHBERG was born in Boston, Massachusetts, on May 10, 1909, and attended Brookline High School and Boston University. During college years he was correspondent for the Boston *Post,* and after graduation joined their sports staff. He left the newspaper in 1952 to become a freelance writer. Since then his articles and non-fiction pieces have appeared in many national magazines, and he is the author of a number of books for adults and young people.